H₂O *surftravelguides*
Costa Rica

1st Edition, second print, September 2008

Published by Jonathan Yonkers Chavarria

D1718559

Author
Jonathan Yonkers Chavarria
buenasolascr@gmail.com

Copy Editors
Alex Gesheva
agesheva@yahoo.com

Janet Raftis
janetraftis@gmail.com

Graphic Designer
Mónica Schultz Clarke
pigati@racsa.co.cr

Map Designer
Hector Gamboa
sapiensgrafica.com

Illustrator
Alex Núñez
artealex.com

Cover Shot
Agustín Muñoz
nitsugaphotography.com

The key to immortality is first to live a life worth remembering.

- Bruce Lee

Photo: Tom Clinton
Surfer: Alvaro Cedeño,
Dominical lifeguard riding a rescue tube.
Location: Dominical

Tamarindo:
653 0404

Samara:
656 0737

fine selections on the beach

ABC
REAL ESTATE

THE SCHOOL

Do it with the best team

Beginner - Ripper
Proper safety & equipment with emphasis
on surf etiquette.
Over 50 years combined experience.
Short & Longboard training.

CHUCKS CABINS

Cheapest, Cleanest,
Grooviest Cabinas in Town
Phone: 643-3328

Other related Booty

CALL FOR INFO
Yacht Surf Charter
Rafting   Canopy   Fishing
Private Photo Session

CONTRIBUTING PHOTOGRAPHERS

Agustín Muñoz
nitsugaphotography.com

Karolina Horniatko
karolinahorniatko.com

Shifi Etteinger
(506) 305 3432
shifisurfshots@gmail.com

Sean Davis
Tamarindophoto@gmail.com

Marcelo Matos
matosfilms@hotmail.com

TWJ Thornton Cohen
nomadpics.com

Tony Roberts
revistacore.com

John Lyman
(506) 658 8106
lymanphoto@aol.com

Joshua López Solano
(506) 818 2350
joshua_2150@hotmail.com

Diego Garcia
(506) 653 1270
bananasurfclub.com

Julia Mueller-Schwenn
artstarproductions.com

Alfonso Petrirena Ortiz
(506) 861 5526
playanegraphotos.com

Orly Apel
orlysurfphoto.com

Ron Allan McLean
dominical.biz
ronalanmclean@yahoo.com

John Mathews
johnmathews11@hotmail.com

Soul Arch Photo
Matt Adame & Jill Parsh
soularchphoto.com

Lance Clinton
surfingringo@hotmail.com

Einav Feit
(506) 360 9848)
einavfeit@gmail.com

Fabian Sanchez
costaricawavehunters.com
minimop@gmail.com

Tom Clinton
tom_clinton@hotmail.co.uk

Paco Salmeron
costaricaway.net

Walter "Teka" Fallas
(506) 758 1016

Rodolfo Sommer
casroma@racsa.co.cr

Henry Aguilera
(506) 839 8542
dominicalsurfadventures.com

Carlos Barrera
rocasurf@hotmail.com

Itai Bar
surfshots@hotmail.com

Melody from Kauai
(No info available)

Andrea Diaz
wavescr.com

Dottie West
dottiewest@yahoo.com

Rafael Garita and friends
rafael_garita@hotmail.com

Randal Ortega Chavez
costaricabirdingjourneys.org

Vili y Josema
No info available

DISTRIBUTION
Jonathan Yonkers Chavarria
buenasolascr@gmail.com

Important note

After March 20th, 2008, in Costa Rica all telephone numbers now have 8 digits. The telephone numbers in this book only have 7 digits. You must add the digit "2" at the beginning of every land-line number and an extra "8" before every cellphone number.

Dedicado a:
Ellibeth Chavarría Miranda y a
Ernesto Zúñiga Ugarte, gracias
por ser los mejores padres del
mundo.

INDEX

Symbols

 Beginners

 Intermediates

 Advanced

 Totally nuts

Abbreviations

- P/B : Private bath
- S/B : Shared bath
- H/S : Hot shower
- Com/kit : Community kitchen

Prices and Choices Listed

All of the choices and prices listed in this book (hotels, restaurants, etc.), are the result of my own personal reaserch. They are not Bible chapters. Use the information I have listed as a way to support your own research. You can start by checking the web-sites or calling the numbers I have provided in order to find out current prices or make reservations.

 High tide

 Medium tide

 Low tide

 Rights

 Lefts

 Rights & Lefts

 Hotels & restaurants available

 No hotels & no restaurants

 Camping rules!

 ATM available

 No ATM available

 Internet available

 No Internet available

 Sandy Bottom

 Cobble stones

 Rocky Bottom

 Nasty Coral

 Willy is hungry!

 Oh my God.. is that a Crock?

 Easy access

 Bumpy roads

 What a mission from hell!

 Party town!

 Family friendly town

 Locals

 Watch your things

About the Author

Jonathan Yonkers Chavarria was born in Ciudad Quesada, Costa Rica on December 22, 1981. Surfing took over his life and soul when he was 12, and he has never regretted it. The addiction has dragged him to Nicaragua, Mexico, Indonesia and Hawaii for punishment and glory, and due to these experiences, he can relate to the surfer's traveling woes and triumphs. Occasionally, the surf gods have allowed him brief respites to travel to Canada, Europe, Thailand and India without his boards, for love and adventure not including waves.

The idea of this book came to mind while holding on for dear life on the roof top of a shady Trans-Sumatra bus.

Currently Jonathan lives near Tamarindo where he directs surf expeditions to the best breaks all over Costa Rica and Central America.

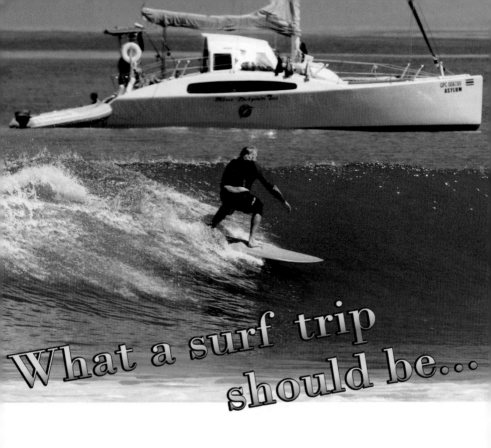

What a surf trip should be...

Blue Dolphin
Catamarans

Tamarindo, Costa Rica
011 (506) 842-3204
tel/fx (506) 653-0867
www.sailbluedolphin.com

2-7 DAY
PRIVATE
CHARTERS

Introduction

Welcome to Costa Rica, our young country blessed with two oceans, abundant natural resources and, most importantly, perfect waves. I invite you to use this book to travel, surf and explore our spectacular coast lines, whether to ride huge round tubes or to chill with your family on a relaxing surf trip.

I have chosen favorite photos from some of the best water photographers in the country to whet your surfer appetite for our varied beach and point breaks and the outer reefs.

This book is equipped with maps of the regions and other practical information that will come in handy when traveling to the surf spots, including the names of favorite local restaurants, popular accommodations, and even some cool local folks you may meet during your trip.

I hope you find this book both useful and enjoyable, and that it helps you come face to face with those incredible waves us surfers were born to ride.

¡Buena suerte y buenas olas!

Jonathan Yonkers Chavarría
La Garita Vieja--Lajas de Matapalo, Santa Cruz, Guanacaste, Costa Rica

WELCOME TO COSTA RICA
WAX YOUR BOARDS!

North Swells
(Nov-Apr)

- Period of clean waves and excellent weather.
- Big epic swells are inconsistent.

Top secret: *seek November, February, March and the last two weeks of December.*

Caribbean Swells
(Nov-April & July)

- Rainy season.
- Bigger swells bomb the Coast more often.

Top secret: *June and July bring amazing waves and weather!*

South Swells
(Apr-Nov)

Key information above has been kindly granted by Dr Omar G. Lizano R. (olizano@cariari.ucr.ac.cr), oceanography professor at CIMAR and Escuela de Física at Universidad de Costa Rica (UCR) in San José, Costa Rica.
Dr Lizano also does studies to determine environmental impact on Central American and Caribbean coasts as part of the information necessary for the development of coastal structures such as marinas, ports, harbors, etc.

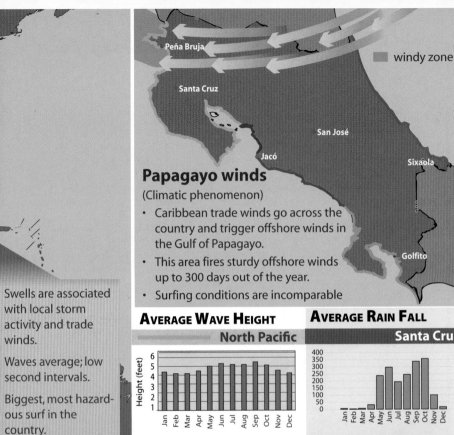

Papagayo winds

(Climatic phenomenon)

- Caribbean trade winds go across the country and trigger offshore winds in the Gulf of Papagayo.
- This area fires sturdy offshore winds up to 300 days out of the year.
- Surfing conditions are incomparable

windy zone

Peña Bruja

Santa Cruz

San José

Jacó

Sixaola

Golfito

Swells are associated with local storm activity and trade winds.

Waves average; low second intervals.

Biggest, most hazardous surf in the country.

Top performers only!

AVERAGE WAVE HEIGHT

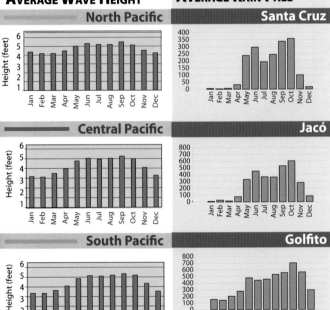

North Pacific

Central Pacific

South Pacific

Caribbean Side

*Source: **Dr Omar G Lizano R.**

AVERAGE RAIN FALL

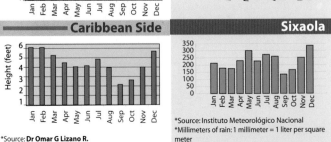

Santa Cruz

Jacó

Golfito

Sixaola

*Source: Instituto Meteorológico Nacional
*Millimeters of rain: 1 millimeter = 1 liter per square meter

Peñas Blancas

Nicaragu

Golfo de Papagayo

Potrero Grande
Roca Bruja

Playas del Coco

Liberia

Arenal

Fortuna

Comunidad

Cañas

Playa Grande
Huacas
Villarreal
Tamarindo
Langosta
Avellanas
Playa Negra
Paraiso
Frijolar

Belén

Santa Cruz

Golfo de Nicoya

Nosara
Ostional
Playa Pelada
Guiones

Península de Nicoya

Sámara

Carmona

Paquera

Puntarenas
Boca Barranca
Caldera
El Hoyo
Orotina

Esparza

San Jos

Santa Teresa
Playa el Carmen
Mar Azul
Malpaís

Cóbano

Isla Herradura

Escondida
Roca Loca
Jacó
Playa Hermosa

Parrita

Esterillos Oeste

Quepos
Playita
Ma
Ant

NORTH PACIFIC REGION
PAG 21

N

0   25 Km
0   25 miles

CENTRAL PACIFIC REGION
PAG 97

COSTA RICAN SURF REGIONS

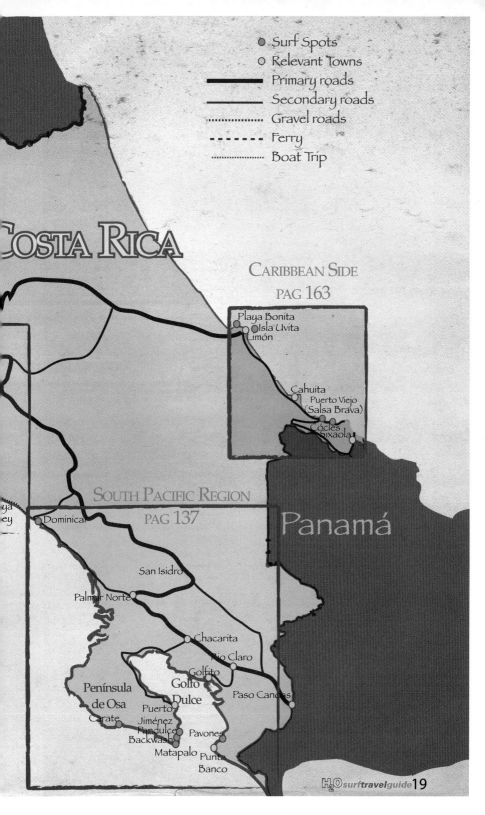

Legend

- ● Surf Spots
- ○ Relevant Towns
- ▬▬ Primary roads
- ── Secondary roads
- ········ Gravel roads
- - - - - Ferry
- ········ Boat Trip

COSTA RICA

CARIBBEAN SIDE
PAG 163

Playa Bonita
Isla Uvita
Limón
Cahuita
Puerto Viejo
(Salsa Brava)
Cocles
Sixaola

Panamá

SOUTH PACIFIC REGION
PAG 137

Dominical
San Isidro
Palmar Norte
Chacarita
Río Claro
Golfito
Golfo Dulce
Paso Canoas
Península de Osa
Carate
Puerto Jiménez
Pandulce
Backwash
Pavones
Matapalo
Punta Banco

Perfection...

North Pacific Region

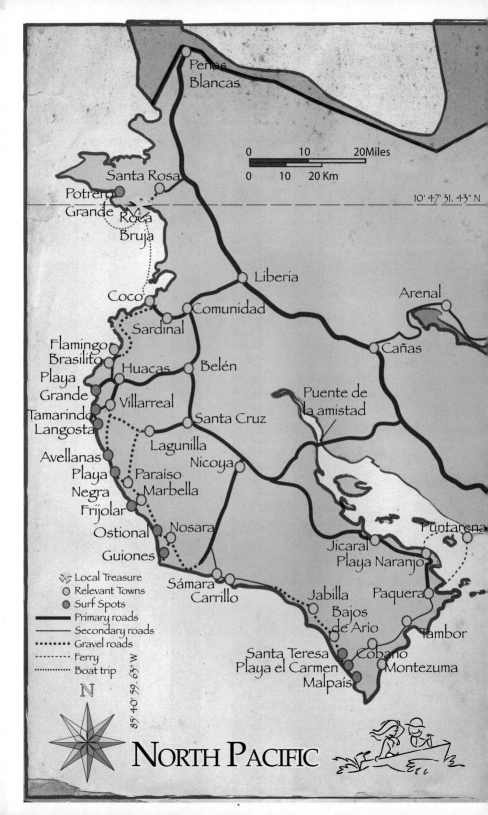

NORTH PACIFIC REGION

This region includes favorite vacation areas for Costa Ricans because of its hot weather and pristine beaches. At the same time, it is famous among surfers for the perfect shaped waves caused by the Papagayo winds. Strong offshore winds that consistently buffet this coast from November to April, The Papagayos brew potent surf magic unmatched in colors and perfection.

The quantity of world class waves found along the coast from Potrero Grande near the Nicaraguan border to Malpaís on the Nicoya peninsula make the region a gold mine for us surfers. We can get lucky with both fantastic surf sessions and excellent weather.

The region is also distinct from the rest of the country as a result of cultural and economic links formed with the neighboring nation of Nicaragua before the province of Guanacaste joined the Republic of Costa Rica in 1825. The best way to experience the wealth of traditions is to attend any of the bull riding festivities (highly recommended!) organized by the local villages around Playa Negra, Tamarindo, Brasilito, etc. during the dry season months.

Photo: Thorton

The Surf

Also commonly known as Ollie's Point, this spot became world famous after the movie Endless Summer II showed surf legends Robert August, Pat O'Connell, Robert "Wing Nut" Waiver, and Costa Rican shaper Marco Pacheco surfing what is probably the smoothest right-hander in all of Costa Rica.

This spot requires a big south swell and dead low tide to break. This, combined with consistent offshore winds that hit the spot up to 300 days out of the year, will create waves that spin flawlessly with machine-like precision for a couple of hundred meters. The walls are not hollow, but they are steep and fast, allowing you to race down the line bottom turning and curving at free will. Old-school long-boarder dudes love this wave; you'll notice their enormous smiles and hyena-like noises as they spray the back of the wave over and over... and over again.

Photo: Carlos Barrera /Surfer: Olger Fernández

Carlos Barrera

The best time to come here is when a solid south swell (preferably 200 degrees or under) matches the days before, during, or after a full moon because the tides will drop a lot lower, gearing the waves with that little extra push that will make your rides unforgettable.

Expect big crowds and bring plenty of sunscreen.

The Place

Potrero Grande is a horseshoe shaped bay with a stunning river mouth located in a hilly desert area of the Santa Rosa National Park. Completely isolated, this place offers no facilities whatsoever. Camping is prohibited.

How to Get There

By boat, Potrero Grande is located in the northern tip of the Santa Rosa National Park near the Nicaraguan border. There is no public access road, and the only way to get there is by boat.

Costa Rica Surf Trips

(www.costaricasurftrips.com) (670 1020 / 670 3810) is a fishermen's association based in Playas del Coco (one hour north of Tamarindo). They are currently the only group with government permits to take people to Potrero Grande and Peña Bruja by boat. You can contact them directly or through the main surf shops in Tamarindo. The standard price is about $320 (plus $6 pp national park entrance fee) for a boat, and includes a full day of surfing Roca Bruja and Potrero Grande, space for 5 people, water and fresh fruit for all.

⌂ Where to Crash

Crash in Tamarindo.

‖ Where to Munch

Since there are no shops or restaurants whatsoever in Potrero Grande, it is highly recommended that you bring plenty of food and water with you for the long boat trip and an energetic surf session. Playas del Coco is the place to grab supplies.

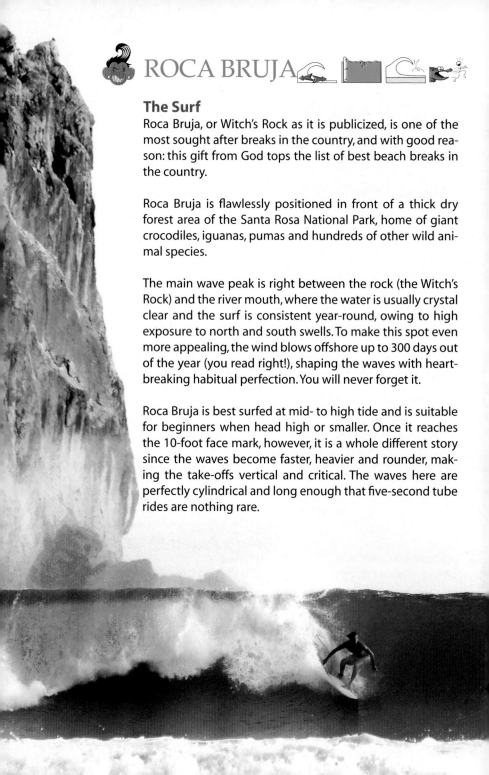

ROCA BRUJA

The Surf

Roca Bruja, or Witch's Rock as it is publicized, is one of the most sought after breaks in the country, and with good reason: this gift from God tops the list of best beach breaks in the country.

Roca Bruja is flawlessly positioned in front of a thick dry forest area of the Santa Rosa National Park, home of giant crocodiles, iguanas, pumas and hundreds of other wild animal species.

The main wave peak is right between the rock (the Witch's Rock) and the river mouth, where the water is usually crystal clear and the surf is consistent year-round, owing to high exposure to north and south swells. To make this spot even more appealing, the wind blows offshore up to 300 days out of the year (you read right!), shaping the waves with heartbreaking habitual perfection. You will never forget it.

Roca Bruja is best surfed at mid- to high tide and is suitable for beginners when head high or smaller. Once it reaches the 10-foot face mark, however, it is a whole different story since the waves become faster, heavier and rounder, making the take-offs vertical and critical. The waves here are perfectly cylindrical and long enough that five-second tube rides are nothing rare.

Photo: Sean Davis
Surfer: Conejo

Photo: Fabian Sanchez
Surfer: Jonathan Yonkers

When the swells approach the beach past the rock, continuous 200-me-ter walls of water are created and they will curl majestically to the left and to the right. When you are taking off you can see this symmetrical process in slow motion, much of it from the inside of the tunnel.

The inside is very vicious on bigger days because of heavy currents. Also, be prepared: the water can get cold (and not just for a Costa Rican!) from November through April due to high offshore winds. So it's a good idea to bring a 2 mm wetsuit just in case. Trust me - you will be glad you did. At dead low tide on a solid north swell, the surf about 600 meters south

of the rock will explode into action. This section of the beach is called El Burro (The Donkey), where tons of boards meet their doom each year riding hollow waves on the shallow sand bar.

The Place

Roca Bruja breaks in front of a majestic rock located in Playa Naranjo, a colossal beach that represents a tiny part of Santa Rosa National Park.

This national park is also of great historical importance because it hosted the Battle of Santa Rosa on the 20th of March of 1856, in which an enemy army led by the great American nutcase William Walker was defeated in its bid to take over the country. The story of William Walker makes excellent reading, and I thoroughly recommend you look it up.

A century and a half later we all go there for the pure pleasure of surfing. And that's how it should be.

How to Get There

By boat
Costa Rica Surf Trips (www.costaricasurftrips.com) (670 1020 / 670 3810), a fishermen's association based in Playas del Coco, is the only group awarded with the 3 daily government permits to take people to Roca Bruja by boat. You can contact them directly or through the main surf shops in Tamarindo. The standard price is about $320 for a boat and includes a full day of surfing Roca Bruja and Potrero Grande, space for 5 people, water and fresh fruit for all.

Take note that only three boats daily can legally go. If you choose to go with anybody but the association, you risk being turned back by the coast guard.

My advice:
Book your boat at Maresias Surf Shop in Tamarindo (653 0224).

By car
SAFARI IRIGARAY (691 0097 / 353 5083), owned and operated by Don Eladio Castro, is the only company I dare recommend for this outrageous drive. Don Eladio Castro, who is an experienced naturalist guide and surfer by heart, has a powerful Land Cruiser equipped with all the necessary gadgets like a winch, chains, chain saws (and I also suspect powerful

magic), to make it to the beach. He arranges transportation, tents and food for his groups. He also hosts university biologists and students who come to the park for biological research.

On your own
Although driving a car on your own is relatively possible in the dry season, I do not recommend you try it. In the wet season the park closes the road entirely, having learned from too many of us who got stuck in the past.

The road connecting the entrance of Santa Rosa National Park to a campsite located in Playa Naranjo, the beach that hosts Roca Bruja, is about 15 kilometers long. Eleven of these are in horrible condition with meter-deep craters, wash-away sections and large fallen rocks. Even with the biggest SUV, I would not recommend you waste your time trying to get there on your own. It is not worth it. Many surfers have been forced to abandon their rented cars deep in the forest because they didn't listen to the advice of locals. Trust me- better, more locally-experienced drivers have tried and failed in emergencies.

By foot

If you still insist on going by land, you can go to Liberia and hire a cab to take you as far as it can go past the park entrance (it won't be very far). From there, you will have to hike about ten kilometers to Playa Naranjo plus four kilometers along the beach to the rock. If you choose this method, be warned that you are committing to a dangerous mission that can make you into forest bait. Plan carefully.

Remember to bring all your water and supplies and pack your trash out with you when you leave. Currently, the park also has strict restrictions on how many people can camp at the beach in Naranjo (call the park office for updates at 666-5051). The campsite is located four kilometers from the spot and has no drinking water or services other than a shower and a basic toilet with a broken door.

Where to Munch

You must bring food with you.

Panadería Musmani (Bakery), located on the left hand side as you approach the main part of Playas del Coco, has some fresh baked goods and coffee. Stop here before you take the boat and buy plenty of food and water for the sail.

PLAYA GRANDE

The Surf

It seems that everybody *knows* about Playa Grande. It seems that every body *is* in Playa Grande, the most crowded spot in the country. But what makes it especially attractive is that when most other spots are completely flat, Grande will have super fun chest-high surf to play with.

During the dry season months with the Papagayo winds and a small or medium size swell (4 to 7 feet), this spot can be absolutely amazing, with turquoise water and perfect A-frame peaks that will break with almond shape and flawless consistency.

Playa Grande on a classic day has numerous pristine barrels: it makes this spot one of the best beach breaks in the country. Naturally, Playa Grande is also the first spot to close out on bigger swells.

In the wet season, it is surfed in the mornings and late afternoons that match medium rising tides. At dead high tide the backwash is quite strong.

Note: Please do not bring *all* of your relatives and *all* of your buddies. Thank you.

The Village

Playa Grande is a 4-kilometer extension of beach with a fair amount of hotels and residential areas that harbor surfers and tourists who want to see leatherback turtles.

How to Get There

By car
From Tamarindo, it should be an easy task: Go to Villarreal and turn left. In Huacas turns left again and follow the signs.

CULTURAL SHORTCUT

From Tamarindo, take a left in Villarreal. Drive 3 to 5 minutes and take the dirt road on the left, after the cemetery. Stop at the next intersection. The guy in the traditional shack on the left corner (his name is Silvanio Rosales) makes very cool surfboard and turtle necklaces out of conch shells and other unusual things. Get one! Ask Silvanio to point out the way. Follow his lead (if he says west!); take the next right for a couple of kilometers and a final left on the main road; keep going west until you get to the waves.

Where to Crash

Although the line up in Grande can be crowded and hostile, the places to stay are rather peaceful and welcoming. It is worth staying at least a night when the waves are firing.

KIKE'S PLACE (653 0834) is on your left when you first arrive in Grande. The owners, Carlos (Kike) Chacon and Yamira Vargas, have a variety of

rooms with and without A/C between $10 and $15 pp, as well as a small pool and the best hangout in town.

PLAYA GRANDE SURF CAMP (playagrandesurfcamp.com) (653 1074), located in the south end of the beach, has rustic, cozy bungalows with a pool, communal kitchen, internet access, A/C or fan for about $10 to $25 pp. Boards, lessons and all inclusive packages are available.

PGI (playagrandeinn.com) (653 0719), next to Rip Jack Inn, has standard, deluxe and apart-

ment rooms for up to 5 people starting at $65+ tax. All rooms have A/C and H/S. They also have a sports bar and a pool.

RIP JACK INN (ripjackinn.com) (653 0480), has clean rooms with A/C, P/B, H/S and a fridge, starting at $75+ tax for 3 people. They also have a fine restaurant with excellent dinner choices.

HOTEL LAS TORTUGAS (653 0423), the hotel that sits right on the spot, starts at around $90 for rooms with A/C and H/S for up to 4 people. There is also a pool, a restaurant, a bar and a Jacuzzi.

Photo: Marcelo Matos
Surfer: Gustavo Strasser

Where to Munch

KIKE'S PLACE serves breakfast, lunch and dinner. The food there is so good and inexpensive that the owners are considered the local heroes.

RESTAURANTE TIERRA DEL FUEGO, close to Kike's, serves great pizza, good wine and typical Spanish dishes; good place to bring your significant other.

LAS TORTUGAS has a restaurant with tasty soups, decent drinks and a refreshing pool and Jacuzzi.

PGI, by the Rip Jack, also has full restaurant service and a pool for relaxing your muscles after surfing. Rip Jack offers a restaurant with a chef and some good dinner choices like seared tuna and other culinary marvels; not too shabby!

THE REAL THING Try the food from one of the local ladies who cooks the real thing that you will not get at any restaurant. Her name is DOÑA IRIABEL. To find her: Drive about three kilometers west of Huacas towards Playa Grande. Once you pass a little bridge, her house will be the second on the left. (If you pass a tiny store on your left, you've just missed it.) It is next to the big palm roof.

Doña Iriabel cooks a whole chicken with veggies, marinated in a typical home-style sauce that is to die for. She

does not speak any English and is not used to having "gringos" come into her house asking for food, so bring someone to translate for you if you don't speak any Spanish, and ask her to cook you a chicken or two. You have to go and order a day in advance so that she can chase the chicken and prepare the sauce. Her brother Delfin also builds palm roofs the old fashioned way… Did I already mention Iriabel is a good cook?

¡Buen provecho!

Surf photography

PLAYA GRANDE SURF SHOP (matosfilms.com) (653 0921), is the one with the concrete wave on the wall, right before Kike's Place, as you arrive into Playa Grande. This shop carries all the surf accessories and gear you could possibly need. Their services, also include, reliable ding repair and professional surf photography. If you had a good session in Playa Grande, chances

40

are you have great surfing pictures of yourself. Stop by their shop and check it out. The top of the line digital equipment and excellent surfing conditions in Grande, make your surf photos well worth the effort.

The Bone Man

Fixing dislocated bones and curing stomach disorders, among other physical problems, by physically manipulating the human body is a tradition passed from generation to generation in parts of the country.

This area has Don Ruben, who lives in El Llano, the next town north of Huacas. He is the local Bone Man.

Many people visit his house on a daily basis to get his treatment. This consists of you biting a piece of cloth and him using his bare hands to put your bones or muscles back in place. Usually the process is very quick, painful and finishes with a loud crack, but, incredibly, it works.

People, including myself, have come into his house (numerous times) un-

Photo: Matosfilms.com

able to walk and left completely new, on their own two feet.

Why am I telling you this? Because a good wipeout can mess you up more than a regular masseuse will be able to fix, and a visit with Don Ruben may save your day. To find him you have to go to the soccer field in El Llano, in the center of the village and drop his name. People will point out the way.

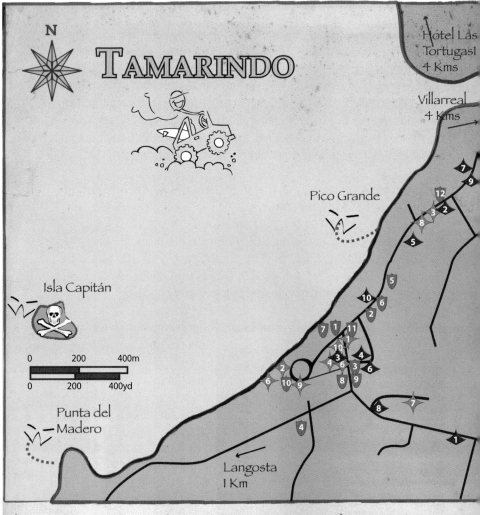

N

TAMARINDO

Hotel Las Tortugas! 4 Kms

Villarreal 4 Kms

Pico Grande

Isla Capitán

0   200   400m
0   200   400yd

Punta del Madero

Langosta 1 Km

♦ HOTELS

1 La Botella de Leche
2 Cabinas Rodamar
3 Cabinas Coral Reef
4 Villas Macondo
5 Cabinas Marielos
6 Domus Kahuna
7 Laguna del Cocodrilo
8 Hotel Pasatiempo
9 Vista Villas
10 Hotel Diria

♦ RESTAURANTS

1 Don Joses's fresh OJ
2 Nogui's
3 Frutas Tropicales
4 Soda Coral Reef
5 Pedro's
6 Urraca's Pizza
7 Dragon Fly Restaurant
8 Coconut
9 Fiesta del Mar
10 Mandarina Juice Bar

🛡 OTHERS

1 Usual bus drop off
2 Info Center
3 Skate park
4 Wayra, Instituto de Español
5 Matos Films
6 Maresias Surf Shop
7 Secret Spot
8 Banana Surf Club
9 High Tide Surf Shop
10 Mambo Bar
11 La Barra
12 Pacific Emergencies

Bananasurfclub

TAMARINDO

The Surf

El Estero de Tama

Photo: Thornton

This is the area in front and south of the river mouth in Tamarindo. Once upon a time there was a solid right hander with fast, hollow walls and perfect barrels there, but those days became distant memories after the sand bar shifted drastically in the early 90's. Locals, including myself, blame all the major developments that may have altered the natural flow of the water that feeds the estuary. Nowadays the waves are gentle most of the year, making the spot one of the best places to learn how to surf in the world.

But be ready: Once every year or two the sand bar reforms for a few days and fires a few indo-like tubes before it goes back into hibernation.

At low rising tides during big swells this place will have super fun, hollow closeouts.

 ## La Isla Capitán

This is the island in front of Tamarindo about a kilometer offshore. Surrounded by a vicious reef, this place gets gargantuan on the biggest NW swells of the year.

Manuel Gonzales, a.k.a. "Tres Pelos", a respected local surfer who still charges this place, ended up in the hospital puking blood with hundreds of sea urchin spikes embedded in his body after wiping out on a big day in La Isla. It is suitable only for experienced bigger wave riders who have the wall nuts to take off in front of exposed rocks where the faces can reach up to three times overhead and break top to bottom.

This spot is surfed at low tide and the best indicator that it is breaking by the book is when Pico Grande is at least 8 feet in the face and reeling. Classic conditions in La Isla are extremely rare and involve surfing massive hollow bombs with crazy drops and unreliable sections from hell.

Obsessive adrenaline junkies should keep an eye open for this wave, but nobody else. You can do the 45 minute paddle to the island from the south end of the bay, or go to Restaurante El Pescador and ask any of the local boat guys for a lift . If you catch it doing what it does best, please send me pictures. I want to see them. Good Luck!

    ## Pico Grande

This is a flaky right-hander that breaks next to the rock in front of Iguana Surf. Most of the year, this spot is just a lame mush ball that breaks

Photo: Fabian Sanchez

45

around the rock and reforms in the inside. However, during big NW and SW swells with high second periods between waves this spot awakens to prove that it can be just as flawless and hollow as Playa Negra. But that will only happen a few times a year.

When the place is on, you will see the outer reefs indicating that the set waves are about to arrive. Once in the outside, the waves suck water out of the sharp reef and jack up, producing round take offs and hollow, blissful sections.

This spot is best surfed at mid-rising tides, and surfing it classic makes you a very lucky person. Pico Grande gets crowded, and it is not a beginner wave. I have had painful experiences getting run over by waves and tossed around into barnacles and sea urchins. Please feel free to learn from my pain. The inside of this spot is Pico Pequeño, a consistent, tiny, hollow and extremely crowded wave.

Photo: Fabian Sanchez

 ## La Punta del Madero

Somewhat mysterious, this spot is inconsistent but powerful, and you can spot it if you stand on the cliff at the south end of the bay in Tamarindo.

La Punta del Madero is usually empty since no one bothers making the 15-minute walk from the main part of town. This spot is only surfed at low tide on a solid NW, SW swell. It can hold solid ten footers that go left and right and break on shallow sections of the anomalous reef, making the rides fast, intense and full of surprises. This is certainly no beginner spot. Bring some friends with you and paddle out through the tiny channel in the first sand section of the beach on the south side of the point. Or, you can jump off the rocks and paddle like hell.

April through August is a good time to surf here, since the southwest swells are quite consistent and the offshore winds are not too strong.

The Town

Tamarindo is the surfer's home base of the North Pacific region with all the convenient facilities (hotels, car rentals, banks, surf shops, etc.) and the surf right out front.

Although the surf can reach epic conditions, all the main spots within the bay are extremely fickle. However, you definitely want to base yourself here while on your hunt for spots such as Peña Bruja, Grande, Negra or Avellanas.

The water is pristine in the dry season and Tamarindo's hot tropical weather and bikinis are its best attractions.

Tamarindo is also an ideal place for learning how to surf, hanging out and meeting people. Note: Tamarindo is protected by a big bay, so when big stormy swells blast the area, it becomes the cleanest place to surf.

How to Get There

By car
Driving to Tamarindo from Liberia' s international airport isn't too hard. Follow the signs to Tamarindo, Hotel Tamarindo Diria or Capitán Suizo. It should only take an hour, whereas from San José it will take you about five hours. Again, the road is well-marked.

By bus
Buses run to Tamarindo from La Parada de Buses de Alfaro (Alfaro's bus terminal 222 2666) in San José, located a short cab ride from La Coca Cola bus terminal. There are also buses to Tamarindo from Liberia's main bus terminal.

By Plane
Tamarindo has a local airport with daily flights from San José and Liberia.

Banana Surf Club

🏠 Where to Crash

LA BOTELLA DE LECHE (labotelladeleche.com) (653 0189) is a hostel located east of Hotel Pasatimpo. The owners have a reputation for being fun hosts and offer dorms with A/C, P/B and lockers for $10 pp. They also have board rentals, lessons and free bicycles for the use of their guests.

CABINAS RODAMAR (653 0109), next door to Frutas Tropicales is traditionally one of the cheapest places to stay. Rooms are simple, with a fan, and start at $10 pp.

CABINAS CORAL REEF (653 0291) is conveniently located near the main street and has simple private rooms and dorms that average about $10 pp.

VILLAS MACONDO (www.villasmacondo.com) (653 0812), waking distance to the town and beach, is a cool little hotel with a pool and clean rooms with a fan and P/B that go from $35 + tax. Rooms with A/C, TV and a fridge are available starting at $55+ tax. They also have a fully equipped kitchen for the use of the guests.

Caminante, son tus huellas
el camino y nada mas;
caminante, no hay camino,
se hace camino al andar.

- Antonio Machado

CABINAS MARIELOS (653 0141), on the main street next door to Iguana Surf, has a pleasant garden, and clean rooms that start at around $40 for double occupancy with a fan. Rooms with A/C, H/S and a fridge are available at extra charge.

DOMUS KAHUNA (domuskahuna.com) (653 0648) has two-bedroom and one-bedroom apartments with A/C, P/B, H/S, fully equipped kitchen, cleaning service and private parking. This place is well maintained and prices start at around $45.

LA LAGUNA DEL COCODRILO (lalagunadelcocodrilo.com) (653 0255), across the street from the Best Western, is a quiet, surfer friendly hotel in front of the Tamarindo estuary. All rooms have A/C, H/S and prices go from $65 for a double occupancy + $10 per extra person. This place has a small lagoon with baby and adult crocodiles fed daily by the owners. It's a good show.

HOTEL PASATIEMPO (hotelpasatiempo.com) (653 0096) has a relaxing atmosphere with hammocks, green areas and cozy rooms with A/C, H/S, and a CD player starting at $80 + tax. Big sporting events are broadcast on big screen TV and they have open mike Tuesdays.

BEST WESTERN VISTA VILLAS (tamarindovistavillas.com) (653 0114) has a glorious view of the ocean and a pool. All the rooms have A/C, T/V, and H/S starting at around $85 + tax. It's a good place to see the sunset and dance on Friday nights.

HOTEL TAMARINDO DIRIA (tamarindodiria.com) (653 0031) in front of the beach, is traditionally one of the nicer resorts in the area. All rooms have A/C and there are two pools and beautiful gardens. Rooms start at around $165 including taxes and breakfast for two.

Where to Munch

NOGUI'S, near the circle, will get you started with massive omelets and delicious, somewhat nutritious waffles.

FRUTAS TROPICALES may easily be the best choice for local food in Tamarindo. They have good breakfasts and the best casados for lunch. They are giant!

SODA CORAL REEF has the cheapest meals in town, and is run by the same family who once ran Soda Rodamar.

PEDRO'S RESTAURANTE, next to Nogui's, is my favorite local place for authentic seafood done local style. Their service is too damn slow and decoration is not the highlight, but the sea food is prepared the way God wills.

The local government is threatening to shut the place down, so if it's still open, eat there, because soon it may just be a memory.

Soda las Palmas in Villarreal serves the best local meals.

Do not miss it!

Photo: Thornton
Surfer: Ricardo Calderón

URRACA'S PIZZA, located at Cabinas Coral Reef has delicious, loaded pizza for under $3. They open during the evenings.

THE DRAGONFLY RESTAURANT (653 0108) (take a left before Pasatiempo) is one of the best restaurants in the area with a fine menu, casual atmosphere and reasonable prices. Make sure you leave room for the chocolate brownie. Making a reservation is a good idea too.

COCONUT, south of Economy Car Rental, is one of the recommended consistent dinner choices in Tamarindo.

FIESTA DEL MAR near the circle is the only 24-hour place in town. Service is not the best but their Tres Leches dessert may make your mouth water at late hours.

Don't Miss!
SODA LAS PALMAS This may well be the best tip for the region in this book. Las Palmas is a buffet-style local restaurant located across the street from the primary school in Villarreal. Doña Epifania Coronado, the owner, cooks all of the typical food choices on a wood-fire stove for about $3.5 a plate, including a natural drink.

When you come back from surfing Grande or Avellanas, stop by for lunch and get fed. Doña Epi is the best.

FRESH OJ: José Manuel Viales sells fresh-squeezed orange juice every morning across the street from Hotel Zullymar. Stop by, before you go surfing, and load up on Vitamin C from the source.

ICE-COLD COCONUTS Dennis Galiano is the deep-voiced man pulling a little cooler on wheels and yelling "Pipas! Pipas!" His ice-cold coconuts are the best refreshment when the heat strikes.

Photo: Mathosfilms.com
Surfer: Alexander Álvarez

Photo: Mathosfilm.com

MANDARINA JUICE BAR Fresh fruit salads with ice cream and fruit cocktails always taste better in the tropics. Stop by Mandarina Juice Bar by Coral Reef and be delighted.

Night Life

Tamarindo has a reputation for having some of the best nightlife in the country. That, of course, depends on the season and the amount of alcohol in the person on duty (you). December to April and spring break usually have the most happening and the most popular bars. The seedy Mambo Bar is the first place where you may want to start looking for action on a regular night. Also visit the Monkey Bar on Fridays and Pasatiempo on Tuesdays. Other new choices like La Barra are popular and fun, but bars in this town change often so you never know. What you can be sure of is a young party-hungry crowd in town. Just ask the locals where to go and you will be sorted out.

Thornton

Ding Repair & Surf Gear

MATOS FILMS (653 0845), next door to UPS, usually has the best deals on new and used surfboards and accessories. He also provides good ding repair, thoughtful surf lessons and professional surf photography.

MARESIAS (maresiassurfshop.com) (653 0224), across the street from Hotel Tamarindo Diria, has a great variety of women's and men's clothing, sandals and fun stickers. Norma, the owner, also has internet, and keeps good local surfers to teach surfing.

BANANA SURF CLUB (bananasurfclub.com) (653 1270) is a cool little shack that offers beautiful surf-artwork and good vibes. They do surf lessons, rent and sell boards and accessories, and design cool T-shirts.

HIGH TIDE (653 0108) is the biggest surf shop in town. They have everything you need as well as everything you don't. They rent out snorkeling equipment, boards and motorcycles.

SECRET SPOT (sstamarindosurf.com) (653 1644), located behind the French bakery, has a good selection on board shorts and cool T-shirts as well as surf lessons and surfing accessories. They have a very cool webpage with a useful swell forecast that's updated daily.

Surf Photography

TWJ THORNTON (nomadpics.com) is an internationally published professional photographer based out of Tamarindo and occasionally Rhode Island. He specializes in documenting adventure travel and wave hunting expeditions by boat, plane and 4WD. He's footage is insane (I'm certainly honored to use some of his shots) and I bet you he is the man to have in the back of your car while surfing awesome waves in scenic places while in Costa Rica.

MATOS FILMS SURF SHOP (653 0845), next door to UPS in Tamarindo, has a photographer in Playa Grande shooting surf sessions on a regular basis and has the daily footage available for display in Tamarindo. The quality of the shots is top.

If you caught a tube or pulled a good maneuver in Playa Grande you know where to buy the CD. Marcelo Matos (owner of the shop) shoots weddings and does surf videos as well.

BANANA SURF CLUB (653 1270) offers professional prints done by Diego Garcia, an experienced photographer who lives in the area and surfs. He usually shoots in the Tamrindo area. Drop by Banana Surf Club and check out his work. He is also available for private sessions.

FABIAN SANCHEZ (costaricawavehunters.com) is a surfer; he is also a photographer and a crazy man! Really, he is crazy. But what better than a crazy surfer photographer to take with you on a crazy surf trip to places like Witch's Rock and Ollie's Point? I wish you could take me, but I don't have the camera or the stamina this dude has.

Medical Emergencies
PACIFIC EMERGENCIES (pacificemergencies.com) (653 8785 / 378 8265), located just south of Best Western Vista Villas, attends all minor and major medical emergencies 24 hours a day. They offer national and international emergency transportation and accept all medical insurances. Their most common job in Tamarindo is to put stitches on beginners who run each other over.

When the Surf Goes Flat

GO SNORKELING Playa Conchal, north of Tamarindo, has clear water with colorful fish for snorkeling. It is not world class, but good for this area.

GO MOUNTAIN BIKING Rent a mountain bike at Blue Trax (east of Pasatiempo) and go to Avellanas through the back roads. It's an awesome trip.

Photo: Matosfilms.com

54

Photo: Shifi

Photo: Shifi

Don Diego is a good man to know in Tamarindo, he is always up to date with the best tours and fun stuff to do in the area.

RIDE A BULL The traditional bull-riding festivities in this region will transport you back to colonial times when men rode bulls and bulls killed men. There is great traditional food and salsa dancing. Ask the locals for updates on the next bull rodeo.

GO SCUBA DIVING Islas Murciélago north of Potrero Grande is one of the best places to dive in the country after Coco Island and Isla Del Caño. For more info, call The Edge at 654 4946 in Flamingo.

GO FISHING: Don Diego from Tamarindo Bay Tours (821 9978) is always updated on the best fishing boats in the region. He also has good contacts for snorkeling and diving.

DO YOGA Daily classes are scheduled at Hotel Arco Iris, north of Hotel Pasatiempo. Drop by to check out the schedules. Some times, traveling instructors also teach martial arts.

OR Book a personalized lesson on the beach with certified Hatha yoga instructor Bathsheba. Phone (506) 342 4940.

For further information on things to do in Tamarindo, visit Costa Rica Paradise (653 0981), next to the main supermarket in Tamarindo.

Thornton

LAS CORRIDAS DE TOROS

Each and every year in this region of the country most local villages organize a traditional annual event between December and April, where the most treacherous bulls in the area are brought into a rustic arena where local men (very seldom women) test their bull-riding abilities for the sake of sport, fame, and love. After each ride, the bull is let loose in the arena for people to play with, though often the bull plays with the people!

Las Corridas de Toros are organized by a different town each weekend and go on all weekend long from 5 to 9 pm, finishing with a nightly dance.

You'll find food, rides, stuff to buy, plenty of cheap beer and everybody is there for the event of the year in that particular town. On Sundays, the best bulls are matched with the best riders in a spectacular competition.

These events are a great window to the traditional culture and customs of the Guanacaste region.

The money raised by the town goes towards the development of the community, usually to the primary school or for road repairs. If you are there at that time of the year, ask the locals where Los Toros will be that weekend - it is a lot of fun and it's for a good cause.

LANGOSTA

The Surf

El Sapo

El Sapo is one of my favorite spots in the Tamarindo area, but it is also very inconsistent.

Go to the beach in Langosta and stand in front of Hotel Barceló. El Sapo (The Toad) is the outside reef to the right of the hotel. If the spot is on, you will know.

The long extension of reef between La Punta Del Madero and the Langosta estuary has a few spots with surf potential, but El Sapo outshines them all with its fast moving walls and long peeling rights and occasional lefts.

December seems to be the beginning season for this wave, but the fact is that it can work any month of the year. Or it can simply not work at all. Do not come to Langosta expecting to surf this spot, but if you happen to pass by during any big swells at dead low tide, take a minute to wait for the set. It may be your lucky day.

Surfer: Giovanni Perini

El Estero de Langosta

This is a river mouth with a sand bar that shifts constantly. The ride is a bit slow with random hollow sections. Fun, but not great.

Since the sand bar shifts all the time, it gets really good when it wants to. The best time to come to Langosta is in the dry season with strong offshore winds, mid-rising tide and a small swell.

If the waves are overhead, they will break in the outside next to a shallow rock and mush their way in to the inside, but if the waves are not very big they can shape up nicely by hugging the random rocks and sand bars in the inside. Then, they barrel with rare perfection and beauty. Once again, you just have to be lucky, or be on speaking terms with the surf gods.

The Place

Langosta is the next beach south of Tamarindo. There are many multi-million dollar houses and a couple of very nice hotels in this area.

How to Get There

In Tamarindo, take a left before Hotel Zullymar and a right after High Tide Surf Shop. The road leads to Langosta.

Where to Crash

SUNSET INN (653 1045) offers great value for your money with clean rooms with A/C, TV, P/B, H/S, and fridge starting at $45 for two people. They also have a swimming pool, ocean view tower and friendly management.

HOTEL CALA LUNA (calaluna.com) (653 0214) is by reputation one of the finest hotels in the area with the best treatment of their clients. Their private villas have A/C and their own pool and start at around $185 + tax.

Photo: Thornton

Where to Munch

HOTEL CALA LUNA has a striking restaurant with excellent dinner choices.

HOTEL CAPITAN SUIZO is not a very surfer-friendly place, but the flavors at their restaurant often are.

Six to Eight & Perfect

I couldn't have been older than fourteen. I had learned to surf in an un-known spot, La Punta, in Playa Brasilito, Guanacaste, and already started to skip school and be "sick" so I could go surfing. I had a 7'6 pint tail Ha-waiian board...a piece of junk that I thought was the hottest ride a man could ever own.

One day Einer (Chilote), one of the first generation surfers (I was just sec-ond generation where I lived) told us youngsters about a lonely place called Avellanas. He made it sound electric: a paradise so remote that busses never went because they had to cross flow-ing rivers and falling trees. Ten of us little mongrels fantasized about one day reaching the mys-terious place with the perfect waves. It became an official chal-lenge and we started to save up for our first surf trip!

59

There we were in a tiny Toyota 1979 pickup truck, almost too many to remember -Adrian & Sergio (Mano-Mano Bros), Carlos, Carlos Luis, Arturo, Eder, Chilote, Chilote's young kid, Douglas, Pan Gato, Victor Julio, one other, and I, hanging off every available grip. Chilote was the only one who stood taller than 5 feet. We started out with surfboards in hands, jugs of water, containers stuffed with Gallo Pinto, a few candles (couldn't afford surf wax then), and 13 of us to push when we got stuck.

Then we were there, except for one important little detail:

A river mouth and crocodiles...

"Just don't fall, ok!?" Chilote kept saying. "Tranquilo, mae, tranquilo!" we would reply. It was like a crowd of monkeys on a match box traveling to Banana Land... rivers, falling trees, huge holes, a little mud here, a little push there; it was fun, it was an adventure. It became new territory for us when we took a short cut through a mangrove forest. The narrow dirt road, the looming mangroves on each side...we were Tarzan on a Toyota. Then we were there, except for one important little detail: We had to swim across a river mouth, and all I could think of was crocs. They bite!

So we left the car and slowly and silently swam across the estuary (without getting eaten) and ran towards the massive sand dune that hid our new surf Mecca. The top of the dune reflected the heat of the morning sun and blurred the sky. The sound of crashing waves became our only guide. First, we saw the spray of a wave. Then a fragment of a beast jacking up and feathering behind the wall of white sand. We didn't know if the waves were good or not but that unmistakable sound of the offshore wind pounding the waves gave us hope.

We made it to the top of the dune and it turned out that Chilote's Avellanas myth was right: massive continuous walls of blue water unfolded in perfect symmetry from left and right ... somewhere between 6 and 8 feet, and perfect.

AVELLANAS

The Surf

 Little Hawaii

This spot is located at the very north end of the beach on the other side of the river mouth. It takes about 20 minutes to get there from Lola's. This right hand point break is best surfed in the wet season months starting in April, when solid south swells make their first appearances. Low tide is the best time to be here, when the reef has better exposure to the traveling swells.

This spot can hold solid double overhead sets or bigger, as long as the swells come from the Southern Hemisphere and not so much from the Northern.

Rides can be intense because the wave is voluminous; some sections can lead you to riding barrels with mutant shapes and others can end you up on the reef pinned to a rock: Choose your own destiny!

I never thought of this spot as dangerous, until the day I got brutally beaten by it after going over the falls.

Beware of strong currents and do not get too comfortable in the inside as clean-up sets are normal.

 ## El Estero de Avellanas

As soon as you mention this name to the locals in Guanacaste you will see big smiles shine on their faces. A lot of us have great memories of this place that involve howling offshore winds and nothing but perfect 10 foot A-frames with long barreling walls of crystal blue water.

This spot is best surfed in the dry season months with a solid NW swell that hopefully will have high second periods between waves. All these factors together will inevitably transform this place into one of the most phenomenal waves on the whole Pacific side.

The A-frame found here when the place goes off makes surfers drool with complete lack of dignity: perfectly hollowed drop, bottom turn, stall, get shacked, come out and scream down the line.

The bottom is rocky, but not sharp. Similar to Little Hawaii, it also breaks best on a dead low incoming tide. At high tide, it becomes fat and mushy. Since this place is very popular with the locals, expect big crowds when on, especially during the weekends and holidays. Play nice!

 ## El Palo

El Palo means" the tree." From Lola's, walk north toward the estuary, and stop at the dead tree with branches pointing towards the ocean.

El Palo is a classic beach break for the North Pacific area due to hollow pristine waves that grind their way to shore. A good size for this spot is 6 or 7 feet. In an El Palo classic, you will find yourself surrounded by perfect little barrels with straight offshore wind and turquoise blue water. When big swells hit Avellanas, this section of

John Lyman

the beach gets grumpy. It's a good time to pull into some of the most senseless closeouts in the region. I love the pathos of this place!

 ## El Parqueo

This is the beach break located in front and north of Lola's. Lola the Pig likes to beach herself in front of this spot. The waves are similar to El Palo but are usually softer and longer. This spot is best surfed during the dry season months when the offshore wind combs its curls with great delicacy and love. This section of the beach does not hold overhead waves very often, but when it does, it does it magnificently.

Caution: you may feel like a wide-eyed child all over again.

John Lyman

 ## La Purruja

When you arrive in the parking lot at Avellanas you will be facing La Purruja. Purrujas are tiny bugs, so small they can barely be seen, that bite you at sun down and have an annoying sting!

The waves in La Purruja are very inconsistent. The best time to surf it is usually in the wet season, with a strong "Pavones" south swell, which is when the waves spin best on the sharp shallow reef. This left-hander has a few connecting sections that curl their way into the inside with a profile that would fit an Indonesian wave.

Catching La Purruja the right way is very rare, and then it can be very crowded. Mid-incoming tide is your best bet.

The Place

Welcome to the most beautiful beach on Planet Earth. Consider yourself privileged for having the chance to visit this small piece of harmony. There is something unexplainable about it. The sand is not blinding white, nor is the water perfect blue. But the welcoming "something" about this place makes it feel without match (at least to me). It may be the smell of the offshore wind, the texture of the ocean, or just something that you can not see but can rather feel. It does not matter, just drop by Lola's, (the bar on the beach named after the giant pig that loves to beach herself on the shore line), order a Margarita pizza and sip on one of their massive tropical smoothies while checking out the waves from the wooden chairs, and you will see what I mean.

Watch for the howler monkeys in the trees though; they happen to share their love with people sometimes, by way of peeing or defecating on them.

How to Get There
By car
There is no regular bus service to Avellanas. You can take a cab from Tamarindo or drive: just take a right in Villareal and follow the signs. In the dry season, a normal trip to Avellanas from Tamarindo can be done in 30 minutes or less. In the wet season, it can easily last an hour. In September and October, the rivers often overflow and do not allow people to drive there at all.

Where to Crash
CABINAS EL LEON (cabinaselleon.com) (658 8318) has rooms for two to three people with orthopedic beds, P/B, H/S and two fans per room starting at $15 pp. They also cater food for their guests.

MAUNA LOA (maunaloa.it) (356 6696) is a beautiful surf resort with a pool, Com/Kit and clean rooms with H/S, orthopedic beds and A/C starting at $30 pp. This is a very good choice.

CABINAS LAS OLAS (658 8315) is the oldest standing accommodation in Avellanas and has a friendly reputation. They have bungalows with a P/B, H/S, a safe, a fan and a balcony starting at $70. This place also has a good restaurant with an open menu as well as internet service and a sweet walkway that leads to the beach through the mangroves.

⫤ Where to Munch

SODA EL MAPACHE, about a kilometer south of Avellanas, serves giant local meals at a local price. The owner is a very friendly lady who cooks good casados.

CABINAS LAS OLAS opens its restaurant from 7 AM to 9 PM. They usually cook good food and you can order breakfast anytime you want.

LOLA'S, right on the spot in Avellanas, has the best pizza on this side of the bushes. The place is a bit expensive, but the food and the location are incredible.

Don't Miss
THE PIZZA AT LOLA'S Pizza this good in a place like this does not happen often in a lifetime. Make sure you spend at least a day in Avellanas.

LOLA THE PIG She (The Pig) is more famous than the president of Costa Rica and often enjoys her popularity by dumping herself on the beach in Avellanas. Do not try to ride her as her knees are a bit deteriorated and she is a pig, not a horse. Have some respect!

PLAYA NEGRA

Photo: Alfonso Petrirena
Surfer: Walter

John Lyman

The Surf

As you may have already seen in the Endless Summer movie, Playa Negra is the wave you travel thousands of kilometers for. The only problem is that there are many others just like you who had the same idea, and you can find all of them (us) shoving each other at the peak at high tide. The crowd factor in Negra is very consistent. The peak has a very small and well-defined takeoff zone and there are always people on it.

This spot is surfed at all tides, but most people are there for high tide. Stay on the beach and wait until surfers get tired and then paddle out. Otherwise, forget it. At low tide, this wave becomes dangerous: the rocks are sharp and there is little water to cushion them. This is also the time when you can accomplish your wildest barrel riding dreams. As the tide gets higher, the bowls fill up with more water and give the wave a better flow.

Playa Negra is very consistent all year round and breaks best on solid NW or SW swells. If you are a beginner, Playa Negra is not for you, period. If you do not like crowds, Negra will never be your favorite wave regardless of the quality. If you like big waves, go to Negra when the swell is enormous. You will have the break all to your lone, lunatic self then.

Photo: Alfonso Petrirena
Surfer: Walter

Finally: From experience, I want you to know that there are other waves that can be just as fun as Negra. If you stop by and see a small crowd, by all means surf and enjoy. If you see a mob of guys fighting to get a wave at the peak, shrug, smile and go somewhere else. You will have a much better time.

The Village

Playa Negra is a beach located 15 minutes south of Avellanas. The main village, Los Pargos, is a fishing town and its soccer field (every town has a soccer field!) is located about a kilometer north of the break.

Negra on a big South West swell with Papagayo winds makes you desire immortality.

Photo: John Lyman

How to Get There

By car
From Avellanas, drive about four kilometers south on the main dirt road. Once you pass the little bridge after the soccer field, take the first right.

By bus
You can also catch a bus to Los Pargos from Santa Cruz, but I wouldn't recommend it.

🏠 Where to Crash
KON TIKI (658 8117), north of the soccer field in Los Pargos, has basic rooms with a fan and two to four beds for $10 pp. They also claim to have the best ceviche in town.

CABINAS UHAINA (658 8178), owned by Manu, Playa Negra's most respected surfer, has a couple of small clean bungalows averaging just over $10 pp. (The entrance is just south of Mono Congo Lodge.)

CAFÉ PLAYA NEGRA (bbplayanegra.com) (658 8351) is located 2 minutes from the break and has six rooms with P/B, H/S, and a fan. The prices range between $15 and $30 pp.

MONO CONGO LODGE (monocongolodge.com) (658 8261), north of the soccer field in Los Pargos, has by far the nicest rooms in the area: A/C, H/S, good beds, and neat, clean wooden floors. The place has a very nice outside deck. Prices start at around $75.

Alfonso Petrirena

HOTEL PLAYA NEGRA (playanegra.com) (658 8034) is impossible to miss as it sits in front of the waves. It offers a pool and huts with space for up to 4 people with a P/B, a fan and a safe starting at around $75 + tax.

Where to Munch

SODA EL MAPACHE, in between Negra and Avellanas, is the cheapest local option for big meals and good service.

CAFÉ PLAYA NEGRA, across the street from La Vida Buena Pizzeria in Los Pargos, is, to my taste, the best restaurant in Negra: good food and a variety of local and international choices at a reasonable price.

Photo: Alfonso Petrireña

PABLO'S PICASSO, on the way to the beach, claims to have burgers as big as your head. They are huge and they are good!

OASIS PIZZA is known for having the best pizza in Negra. The place is clean and friendly and the pizza is definitely tasty.

LA VIDA BUENA, by the main entrance to the beach, is a local bar that does serve food, but is mostly a night-time hangout.

Don't Miss

DESSERT IN CAFÉ PLAYA NEGRA. They usually have something different but always very tasty.

Surf Photography

JOHN LYMAN PHOTOS (lyman-photo@aol.com) (658 8106) is the man with the straw hat and the big zoom lens. He shoots high-resolution digital photography and is also available for private sessions. If you surfed a good day in Negra, chances are he will have good shots of you. He is also the man to talk to for shooting your wedding in this area.

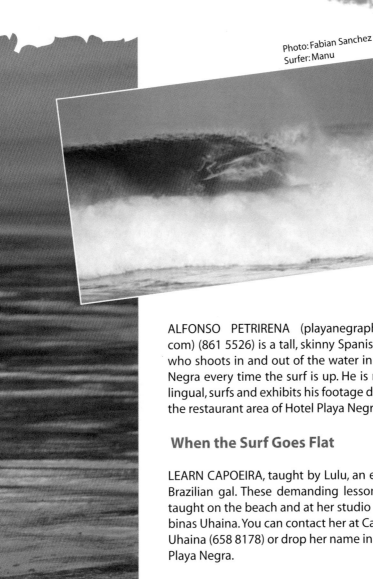

Photo: Fabian Sanchez
Surfer: Manu

ALFONSO PETRIRENA (playanegraphotos. com) (861 5526) is a tall, skinny Spanish guy who shoots in and out of the water in Playa Negra every time the surf is up. He is multilingual, surfs and exhibits his footage daily in the restaurant area of Hotel Playa Negra.

When the Surf Goes Flat

LEARN CAPOEIRA, taught by Lulu, an expert Brazilian gal. These demanding lessons are taught on the beach and at her studio in Cabinas Uhaina. You can contact her at Cabinas Uhaina (658 8178) or drop her name in Hotel Playa Negra.

HAVE A MASSAGE Lulu also offers professional massage services at a fair price. Your back will be grateful.

TALK TO JAVIER (3582038), also known as El Conde Galier. He is a very experienced mountain and water guide and will focus your attention far away from the beaten tourist path.

PLAYA FRIJOLAR

The Surf

Frijolar is a fun beach break, with great potential, located about an hour south of Negra. In classic conditions, the waves are hollow with explosive barrel sections, but those conditions are rare to come across because of wave's high sensitivity to the wind and shifting sand bars. Frijolar also has poor ability to hold bigger swells.

Frijolar hosted the only shark attack reported by a surfer in Costa Rica (at least that I know about). Rossell Menking got over 300 stitches after being accidentally bitten by a shark while wading in knee-deep water. He is lucky the shark didn't really mean it.

Local surfers Ricardo "Rastin" Calderón and Geinner "Flash" Miranda from Tamarindo also had a frightening experience after jumping in the water from a boat, without realizing that 8-foot sharks were feeding right next to them. Fortunately they made it back to the boat unharmed.

According to local fishermen who constantly get the evidence stuck in their nets, the beaches between Negra and Ostional are heavily shark infested. The reason for this is unknown, but the water in this area of the country is oddly colored and has a fishy smell.

The Place

Frijolar is a lonely beach between Negra and Ostional (in the middle of nowhere). The closest village is Marbella (700 meters east of the beach), which has a soccer field, a soda and a few small grocery stores.

How to Get There

By car

From Playa Negra you must head south towards Paraiso and follow the signs to a village called Marbella. The trip there from Negra may take 45 minutes to an hour and a half depending on the road conditions. Once in the village, turn right after the public telephone box (there is only one).

By bus

There is daily bus service to Ostional from Santa Cruz. These buses must stop in Marbella. This hot and bouncy vomit comet takes nearly 3 hours on a good day and you will have to ride in a dusty road full of chickens. Not recommended.

🏠 Where to Crash

CAMPING

There is a campground right on the beach owned by an Italian couple. They have showers, bathrooms and a wood stove you can use.

▌ Where to Munch

Soda Bella Mar, run by Miriam Córdoba in the north end of the soccer field in Marbella, always has good breakfast and lunch with good fruit shakes at a low price.

 OSTIONAL

The Surf

Beach breaks and more beach breaks! Ostional is one more on the long list of high standard beach breaks in Costa Rica. Mid-rising tides by the soccer field where you need to be if you reach this godforsaken area of the world. The lonely dusty roads that connect this town to the rest of the region (they seem never-ending!) keep this area from developing like other areas such as Tamarindo, but its long classy waves still make this place an attractive choice for core surfers seeking a good thrill. At high tide the spot becomes mushy, and at low tide the waves close out. So, integrating the right tides with the morning sessions is your best formula to score clean tubes in Ostional.

It is important to know that this beach is a Wildlife Shelter (federally protected area) where literally hundreds of thousands of sea turtles take over the beach once a month, especially from July to December, to lay their eggs. This event is locally known as "La Arribada" (The Arrival), and during Arribadas surfing is NOT ALLOWED, no matter how good the waves may be. One more factor to consider is that the young surfer community that blooms in this town is not adjusting well to the new crowds publications like this damn book seem to attract, so I recommend you leave your ego at home and surf this place with high surfer's common sense.

The Village

Ostional is a very small, nearly isolated, dusty (or muddy) village that is most commonly known for the monthly arrival of hundreds of thousands of turtles that come to the beach to lay their eggs on the sand.

How to Get There
By car
In the dry season you can drive south on the road from Playa Frijolar. The trip may take you 45 minutes if the road is in good condition. Or you can drive in from Nosara through Nicoya.

By bus
You can also catch a 3.5-hour bus ride from Santa Cruz (Just Say NO!). Either way, be warned that during the rainy months of May, September and October, the numerous creeks along the way usually turn into flooding rivers that often leave this area completely isolated.

Where to Crash
CABINAS LA GUACAMAYA (682 0430) has fairly clean basic rooms right near the waves for well under $10 pp. Doña Rosa, your host, also has a grocery store with basic supplies.

CABINAS OSTIONAL (682 0428), in front of Soda La Plaza, has simple rooms with a fan for under $10 pp.

Where to Munch
SODA LA PLAZA, by the soccer field, is open for breakfast, lunch and dinner. This is the best option in town. For more meal options go to Pelada or Guiones.

Arts and Crafts
MIGUEL ZUÑIGA (811 2759), a local surfer in the village, makes striking necklaces and crafts out of shell and bull horn. Drop his name in the village and check out his stuff. He lives just south of Cabinas La Guacamaya.

Photo: Rafael Garita and friends

NOSARA

Nosara does not have waves. It is only a reference point.

The Village

Nosara is a small village 5 kilometers northeast of Guiones and is not on the ocean, so no waves there. However, this little town is a good point of reference for this area and it has a small airport, inexpensive restaurants and a doctor. I have my reasons for sending you there.

How to get There
By car
In the dry season you can drive from Tamarindo along the coastline. Just read the signs carefully and you will be fine. In the wet season, starting in May, you are better off going through Belén, Santa Cruz and Nicoya.

By bus
Alfaro (Bus Company) (222 2666) runs buses from San José to Nosara, leaving at 6:00 AM (call to confirm the time). From Tamarindo you must take a bus to Santa Cruz, from there one more to Nicoya, and from Nicoya another one to Nosara.

By plane
Nosara has a local airport with daily flights from San José.

Where to Crash
CABINAS AGNNEL (682 0142) is the best (least shady) local accommodation with simple rooms with a fan for under $10 pp.

Where to Munch
RANCHO TICO, on the corner after the Airstrip a good restaurant with a wide-ranging menu and low prices.

LA CASONA, on the corner before the Airstrip also has very good food at great prices.

Medical Emergencies

CENTRO MEDICO DE NOSARA (682 0460), by the hardware store, has a doctor in case you are hurt and need professional care.

THE RED CROSS (682 0175) (by the soccer field), works in conjunction with the 911 emergency system. They can offer emergency transport to the nearest Hospital in Nicoya, about 2 hours away.

PLAYA PELADA

The Surf

This attractive beach has great surf when the conditions that result from big stormy south swells allow. This does not happen very often, so *tranquilo mae*. Pelada is more for hanging out. Drop by and have a drink, relax. Life is good. The main wave is a right that breaks off some rocks in front of the beach access. In big swells, when Guiones is closing out, this spot may be the best way to go. But keep your eyes open for hints that giant swells may give. LOOK AROUND, pay attention, and you may get lucky!

The Village

More than a regular surfer beach, Pelada is a local fishermen's hang out, with families who come to enjoy sun and sand on weekends.

How to Get There

Pelada is just a 5 minute drive north of the neighboring Playa Guiones.

REFUGIO DEL SOL (refigiodelsol.com) (682 0287), just walking distance to the beach, has four warm new rooms and one apartment. Prices range between $30 and $50 per room per night with H/S and a fan.

HOTEL RANCHO SUIZO (nosara.ch) (682 0057) is located on the street behind The Red Lion. It is well maintained; the rooms with H/S and a fan start at around $55 for two people and include breakfast.

PANCHO'S RESORT (panchosnosara@racsa.co.cr) (682 0591) has a pool and rooms with A/C, and a fridge. Prices go from $65 to $140 depending on the room.

HOTEL PLAYAS DE NOSARA (nosarabeachhotel.com) (682 0121) is the giant castle-like building up on the hill in the south end of Pelada. Prices start at $90. The view from the hotel and the crazy architecture make this place an interesting splurge.

Where to Munch

OLGA'S BAR RESTAURANTE, located right on the beach, is a local hang with cheap food, cheap beer and free bocas. They are open for breakfast, lunch and dinner.

THE RED LION, on the main road to the beach, is a good place for breakfast; they also serve lunch and a daily BBQ dinner. They have a pool table, darts and good vibes. They close on Tuesdays.

PANCHO'S, also on the main road to the beach, is a local choice (the only choice) for Mexican food in Pelada.

RESTAURANTE EL PELICANO, located inside of the Rancho Suizo Hotel, is a high standard restaurant with well-prepared dinners and quiet atmosphere.

PLAYA GUIONES

 The Surf

Guiones is a long extension of beach break that attracts a lot of swell. A classic day in Guiones translates into endless lines of swell that dump long, peeling, powerful waves into the deep sand bars. Low tide is best for us potato-chip riders because the waves jack up on the sand bars and drive their way into the beach with a lot of push and some random hollow sections. High tide is best for long boarders and beginners as the waves become slower and softer. (Unless it is big, this is not rare.) The beach break in Guiones is very similar to the one in Santa Teresa. From March to July the waves in this spot can be predictably overhead and move a lot of wa-

ter, so heads up, insane paddling is often involved. This area of the Nicoya Peninsula is not blessed with the consistency of the dry season offshore winds that strike Tamarindo, but sometimes...

Wow!

Get up early in the mornings to reap the greatest rewards.

The Village

Also known as "The Project", Guiones is a huge extension (over 1000 hectares) of land in front of Playa Guiones that was purchased by an American investor in the 70's. Today, The Project is a giant residential area with a majority of North American inhabitants living in it. This village has far more real state offices than local restaurants and decent surf shops combined.

This I find quite ridiculous. Guiones is certainly not my favorite hang out. But, I like the waves and I love the beach.

How to Get There

Guiones is also referred to as "Nosara" by the local Gringos. So before asking directions, think who you ask first. Its real name is Playa Guiones.

By car
To get to Playa Guiones from Tamarindo, for example, you can drive on the road that goes along the coastline. Expect two to three hours. But this is only recommended between the months of December to April. Otherwise try the road through Nicoya, which will take you about the same time.

By bus
Same as for Nosara, but you have to ask the bus driver to drop you off in Guiones.

🏠 Where to Crash

SOLO BUENO HOSTEL is on the north side of Guiones, north of the Delicias Del Mundo grocery store. Their bunk beds go for about $12 pp and include the use of a kitchen. Camping is also possible. This place is cool.

TIKI SURF CAMP (682 0217) west of the Delicias Del Mundo grocery store, has a shared rancho with single beds for around $15 with a fan and a shared H/S. Camping is also available. This place is tranquilo and is within walking distance of the beach.

BLEW DOGS (blewdogs.com) (682 0080) is a surfer's complex with dorms and private rooms that go from $10 to $90 depending on your choice. They have a pool and a restaurant.

CASA TUCÁN (safarisurfschool.com) (682 0113), located by the main entrance to the beach, has a pool and clean rooms with A/C and H/S starting at $65 + tax.

CAFÉ DE PARIS (cafedeparis.net) (682 0087) in front of Coconut Harry's, has nice rooms with A/C and hot shower starting at $70 + tax. They have a small bakery with good sweets.

HARBOR REEF LODGE (harborreef.com) (682 0059) is well placed near the beach. Prices for rooms with A/C, H/S and a fridge start at $80. Also contact them for house rentals in the area.

Where to Munch
SODA TICA, next to National Car Rental, is unmatched in town when it comes to local inexpensive food. Unfortunately, it is closed on Sundays. (For more cheap choices, check out the Nosara section.)

BLEW DOGS has hamburgers and other gringo-style food choices to please American surfers who miss having trash inside of their bellies. Casa Tucán serves a tasty breakfast; located near the beach.

MARLIN BILL'S, by Coconut Harry's, has a panoramic view of the ocean that works well with a good afternoon lunch or an early dinner with some Margaritas.

Ding Repair & Surf Gear
JOHAN MENDEZ (cell 822 2303 / 682 0328 home) is the most experienced local ding repairman in Guiones. He usually hangs out at Coconut Harry's Surf Shop where there is board rental and basic surf supplies.

NOSARA SURF SHOP (682 0186), on the main road to the beach, has a wide variety of boards for rent and sale and is the best equipped surf shop in Guiones.

to: Julia Tropix

Surf Photography

SOUL ARCH PHOTO (soularchphoto.com) (682 0226) Matt Adame and Jill Parsh are the people you want to talk to if you want some good memories on a CD. They have a place west of Café de Paris, next door to Robin's Ice Cream. The best place to find them is on the beach in the early mornings. They also have waterproof casing for their cameras so you may see Matt in the water.

When the Surf Goes Flat

GET A MASSAGE Tica Massage (682 0096) by Casa Tucán has a group of professionally trained local lassies giving excellent massages at a fair price. From someone who's had one, they're great!

HAVE A COCKTAIL Bar Luna, located in Playa Pelada, is a cool place right on the beach where you can drink your flat spell troubles away.

TAKE A DAY TRIP Playa Carrillo, north of Samara, is a very attractive beach with a small village. Check it out.

Photo: Orly Apel
Surfer: Thomas Ritchie
Location: Santa Teresa

SANTA TERESA

The Surf

Santa Teresa

This is an area outfitted with the best beach break waves around. I describe Santa Teresa as good (as in not mind-blowing as Hermosa or Peña Bruja), but it is definitely great enough to put you through the spin cycle. Depending on the swell direction and the positioning of the sand bars, there will be longer rights or longer lefts. The latter curl better on SW swells.

Similar to most beach breaks on the Pacific side of the country, Santa Teresa closes out on big south swells that usually come in late in the wet season, and stays small and inconsistent in the early months of the dry season. The period between February and August usually maintains a good balance between wind and swell consistency. Santa Teresa also gets ungodly big at times – one of the biggest beach breaks in the country, and after the tourist boom one of the most crowded ones as well. The best conditions are during small or medium size swells (4-7 feet) at lower tides (it turns mushy at higher tides), in the dry season months, when the Papagayo winds are strong enough to share their blessings even here. This does not happen as often as it does in the northern part of the Nicoya Peninsula, in places like Avellanas or Playa Grande. Some of the favorite breaks are right in front of Seneida's and Point Break, but the whole beach is equally good. Just look for an empty section and surf it.

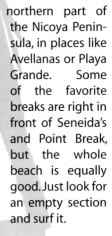

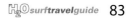

The Village

This is the current frontier in Costa Rica for a laid back atmosphere, white sandy beaches and good waves. The simple lifestyle that once made Costa Rica famous still remains untouched on the dusty roads and lush surroundings of the area (Santa Teresa, Playa del Carmen and Malpaís). The waves are consistent all year around, and the rustic infrastructure blends well with the hippie and surfer crowds that the area attracts.

The tourism industry recently entered a boom, so making a reservation for a place to stay prior to arrival may be a practical initiative.

How to Get There

Santa Teresa begins about two kilometers north of Playa del Carmen. Refer to the instructions on reaching Playa del Carmen.

Where to Crash

CUESTA ARRIBA (640 0607) has clean spacious dorms with a P/B, com/kit, lockers, surf racks, and lounge area for $10 to $12 pp including coffee and toast in the morning. They also have tons of movies to watch.

CASA ZEN (zencostarica.com) (640 0523) is a friendly colorful place with a Thai restaurant. Dorms and private rooms average $12 to $20 pp with S/B and com/kit. Camping is also possible.

HOSTEL BRUNELA (640 0321) has dorms with P/B, lockers, com/kit and lounge area from $8 to $12 pp. Beginner surfers get a surfboard rental and a surf lesson for free (so claims the owner).

SENEIDA'S (640 0118) was one of the first places in Santa Teresa, located right in front of the best peak and with a staff that is as local as it gets. The rooms vary between $13 pp with S/B, and $20 pp for a fully equipped little surf shack. Seneida's is also one of the best places to camp, offering lockers and security in the dry season months. Local food is available as well.

POINT BREAK (surfing-malpais.com) (640 0190) is also located on the beach, next door to La Lora Amarilla. There are rooms with a shared bath and privates with a kitchen, all averaging around $20 to $30pp.

RARATONGA (640 0475) is a brand new hotel run by an Italian couple. They have rooms with and without a kitchen for 2 to 4 people. All rooms have A/C, H/S, P/B and a fan and average around $30 pp including taxes, breakfast, laundry service and daily room cleaning.

Where to Munch

SUGAR MAMI'S PAPIS, specializes in healthy food and good portions.

Their solid wraps, salads and pastries are to die for. You can eat here, go across the street and hit the best waves in the area.

JUNGLE JUICE is a popular eatery with a healthy menu based on fruit, veggies and fresh fish. Closed after brunch for surfing! Open again after surfing! You will not know how good it is unless you drop by.

PIZZA TOMATE is a consistent food source. I think the Tomato, sauce they cook is perfect! I personally enjoy Calzones the best.

QUE TAL BURGERS How about a huge tuna burger for dinner after an afternoon surf session? I recommend you consider that.

Don't Miss
RESTAURANTE LANGOSTA PARAÍSO, in Manzanillo (4 Kilometers north of Santa Teresa) is where the locals go to eat the best ceviche in the country. Remember that a good ceviche must always be paired with an ice cold beer.

LA COCINA DE LEÑA LA COBANEÑA in the town of Cobano serves an appetizing arroz con camarones (fried rice with shrimp): Good food just tastes better when cooked on a wood fired stove by a small-town woman.

RESTAURANTE RARATONGA (640 0475), located upstairs in Raratonga hotel, is a very casual restaurant with a pleasant vibe and some of the tastiest typical Italian dishes you can try outside of Italy. The menu is based on fresh ingredients and home made recipes. This place is open for dinner and only during the high season months.

Ding Repair and Surf Gear
KINA SURF (640 0627), next door to Jungle Juice, has a good variety of surf boards and surf accessories. The Kiwi owner, like most proper Kiwis, is a friendly fellow who loves to surf. You can also contact him for surf instruction.

Surf Photography
JULIA TROPIX & 360° SURF SHOP, (artstarproductions.com) (643 0369), located in the Brunela complex, is where you can go for high resolution photography. Julia, the owner, who is easily found taking photos in Santa Teresa, where the waves are best, also has a surf shop with all the goods, including surf boards and accessories.

ORLY APEL (orlysurfphoto.com) (640 0169), is a cheerful lady who can be found with her tripod and top of the line camera equipment in Playa el Carmen. Talk to her about sharing private sessions with your friends. The results will be highly rewarding. She usually exhibits her work at Artemis Cafe across from Frank's Place.

The Surf

El Carmen, in front and around is a softer version of Santa Teresa. The waves are rather fat, slow and soft in comparison. But when conditions miraculously coincide, the waves definitely rise to meet the standard of a high quality beach break. The good thing about this spot is that it breaks best at higher tides, offering the much-appreciated gift of having a place to surf at all times in the area. There is a good restaurant right in front; so drop by, hang out, have a drink and take it easy.

The Village

Playa El Carmen is the center of all the action; this is where you get on and off the bus and where most businesses are located (including Frank's Place, the unofficial bus station). It's all very convenient if you want to party and be in the middle of all the surf spots. Santa Teresa starts about two kilometers north of Frank's Place and Malpaís starts just south of Frank's Place.

How to Get There
By bus
From Tamarindo, doing it on the public buses takes for ever. Trust me, it is not worth it. CR Paradise (653 0981) in Tamarindo, offers direct shuttles that will save you time and hassles.
From San José, there are two to four daily buses leaving from La Coca Cola Station. These buses go direct (call 642 0992 or 389 7177 for latest schedules).
From Jacó, catch a bus to Puntarenas, a cab to the ferry terminal and once in Paquera, finish the trip on the local buses. Most buses and private shuttles will drop you off at Frank's Place, in Playa el Carmen. Staying here works if you are a beginning surfer. If you are seeking stronger

waves, how ever, I say you go to Santa Teresa at once. Take a cab or hop on the local bus which connects Malpaís and Santa Teresa. It drops you off at Tano Gas (unofficial gas station), there are excellent accommodation choices near there (use the map in Malpaís section).

By car
From Tamarindo: In the rainy season, you must drive through Santa Cruz, Nicoya, Jicaral, Paquera, and Cobano. This trip will take no less than 5 hours. In the dry season, starting in mid-December when the Bongo River will allow it, you can go on the back roads passing by Nosara, Camaronal, Punta Islita, Coyote, Ario, Manzanillo, Hermosa and finally Santa Teresa. This is one of the most spectacular drives in the country. It's a good idea to spend a night or two along the way in Guiones or camping somewhere along the road at an isolated beach break (there are hundreds of them!). From Jacó, you must drive to Puntarenas (1 hr) and take the ferry across to Paquera. (Make sure you get on the Paquera ferry, and not on the Naranjo one). From San José, the quickest way to go is on the Pan-American Highway through San Ramón and Esparza. Follow the signs to Puntarenas.

By plane
There is a local airport in Playa Tambor with flights from San José. Ask travel agencies all over the country for more info. Tambor is a good 30-minute ride from Santa Teresa.

Ferry Schedules
Puntarenas-Paquera Departing at 6:30 AM, 10:30 AM, 2:30 PM, 6:30 PM, 10:30 PM.
Paquera-Puntarenas Departing at 4:30 AM, 8:30 AM, 12:30 PM, 4:30 PM, 8:30 PM.
Note
Call the ferry office to confirm the schedule above at 641 0515. Ferries take about one and a half hours and are equipped with a bar. Taking the late ferries with the stars above you and a drink in hand is not too shabby at all!

🏠 Where to Crash
CABINAS PLAYA EL CARMEN (640 0179) has simple rooms with the basics (a bed and a fan), shared bath, and a community kitchen for just under $10 pp. They also have a soda with local food.

TRANQUILO BACKPACKERS (tranquilobackpackers.com) (640 0589), is a fun choice near the beach. Their dorms and double rooms include free breakfast and internet with Skype, starting at $10. I also like their Hostel in San José.

Photo: Orly Apel
Rider: "Don Piano"

CABINAS SURF PARAÍSO (640 0013) has two-bed rooms with hot shower, fans and a kitchen for up to 4 people for $60-$80 including tax. Food is also available.

HOTEL DEL PACÍFICO (640 0285) has clean rooms with A/C for $50 for 3 people. Fridge and TV are available at additional charge.

RANCHOS ITAUNA (ranchos-itauna.com) (640 0095) is conveniently located in the middle of Santa Teresa and Playa El Carmen. The lodging consists of open hut-style bungalows with fans and private bath for $70 for two people and an additional $10 per extra person, rooms with a kitchen available at extra charge. The owners run a good restaurant with Brazilian food and occasionally throw Ko Phangan style full-moon parties on the beach, with DJs and giant speakers… Buenísimas!

FRANK'S PLACE (640 0096) This is the center of it all. More than just a hotel or a restaurant, Frank's Place is a local institution, the first on the scene. Rooms are available between $25 and $50 pp, depending on the room, and include a pool and a Jacuzzi. Frank's Place is also the unofficial bus station. Buses going or coming from Cobano, Paquera and San José stop here. There is also an ATM machine, internet, travel agency and liquor store—all the amenities.

⫼ Where to Munch

FRANK'S PLACE serves consistent good food all day long. The seafood soup served here may well be the best in all of Costa Rica.

PIZZERIA PLAYA EL CARMEN is the only restaurant where you can eat and check out the waves at the same time. Don Carlos and his wife Yerlin serve great pizza, salads and pasta. Their best item is the garlic dressing for the pizza that sits on the tables. Good place for lunch.

Ding Repair and Surf Gear

ALEX'S SURF SHOP (640 0364), next door to Cabinas Charlie's, is the only local-owned surf shop in town. His shop is basic, but he does ding repair and has all the basics like wax, leashes, fins and surf lessons.

When the Surf Goes Flat

GO FISHING OR SNORKELING Local fishermen are based in a small harbor next to the Sunset Reef Hotel. Talk to them directly about going fishing or snorkeling -- there is a lot of tuna in this area and they know where to look.

RENT A QUAD There are hundreds of kilometers of dirt roads and beaches to explore south of Santa Teresa. Please slow down when you see children on the road.

JUMP OFF A WATERFALL There are impressive waterfalls that you can jump from in Montezuma. Regardless of the waves, take a day to check this place out. Bring food and dippers. A lot of people have died after jumping unsuccessfully from the first waterfall so, needless to say, stay away from the first one. The second and third falls have good jumps and a rope swing.

CHECK OUT THE CROCS IN THE BONGO The Bongo River, north of Santa Teresa, has tons of crocodiles hiding deep in its thick mangroves. For more info call Guido Saenz at 824 6845.

89

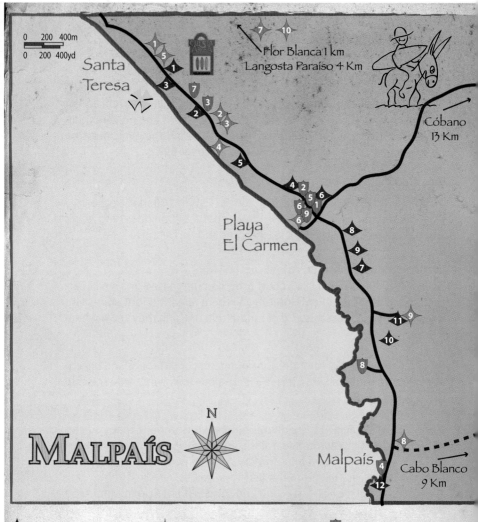

Flor Blanca 1 km
Langosta Paraíso 4 Km

Cóbano
13 Km

Santa
Teresa

Playa
El Carmen

N

MALPAÍS

Malpaís

Cabo Blanco
9 Km

0   200 400m
0   200 400yd

HOTELS

1 Cuesta Arriba
2 Hostel Brunelas
3 Seneida's
4 Tranquilo Backpackers
5 Ranchos Itauna
6 Frank's Place
7 Malpaís Surf Camp
8 The Place
9 Oasis
10 Moana Lodge
11 Vista de Olas
12 Sunset Reef Hotel

RESTAURANTS

1 Sugar Mami's Papi's
2 Jungle Juice
3 Pizza Tomate
4 Que Tal Burguers
5 Restaurante Raratonga
6 Pizzería Playa el
   Carmen
7 Flor Blanca
8 Mary's
9 Vista de Olas
10 Langosta Paraíso

OTHERS

1 San José Bus Stop
1 Bank
1 Internet
2 Alex's Surf Shop
3 Kina Surf Shop
4 Local fishermen
5 Great ceviche!
6 Quad rentals
7 Unofficial gas station
7 Local Bus Stop
8 Hotel Mar Azul
9 Doctor

MALPAIS

The Surf

 Mar Azul

This fun but inconsistent point break is located in Malpaís, in front of the hotel/restaurant of the same name. There are far better chances for a fresh ceviche and a cold beer than there are for surfing raging waves. Mar Azul is a long left of great potential, and it breaks far outside in two different sections that can connect and create outstanding rides. Usu-ally this place gets good on huge SW swells, like the ones that usually

Playa Santa Teresa

Photo: Orly Apel

Playa El Carmen

Photo: Julia Tropix

Photo: Orly Apel

Matosfilms.com

Playa Malpaís

make the entire beach break in Santa Teresa close out. That is also why this spot can also be very crowded when the choices of places to surf narrow down to the point breaks that can hold the size, or are not as directly exposed to the open ocean swells. The latter choice is the case in Mar Azul.

This area of town is isolated and beautiful.

The Village

Malpaís is a sleepy fishing village located south of Playa del Carmen. This quiet area is where most of the nicest places to stay are located and where Mar Azul is to be found.

How to Get There

Malpaís begins just south of Frank's Place. Mar Azul is halfway along the 4 kilometer road; look for the hotel sign with the same name.

Photo: Julia Tropix

🏠 Where to Crash

MALPAÍS SURF CAMP (malpaissurfcamp.com) (640 0031) ranges from clean simple rooms with a fan and S/B for $45 + tax for 4 people to more equipped villas and casitas that start at $105 + tax for 2 people. They have friendly staff, a bar, and a pool.

THE PLACE (theplacemalpais.com) (640 0001) is a small hotel with modern-rustic architecture, a pool and chill atmosphere. Rooms vary from $50 + tax for 2 people, to $180 + tax for rooms for 5 people. They have movie nights by the pool once a week.

OASIS (nicoyapeninsula.com/malpais/oasis) (640 0259) has comfortable rooms for 2 people with good beds, hot showers and well equipped kitchens, at around $65 + tax.

MOANA LODGE (moanalodge.com) (640 0230) is an exotic hotel of "comfort and style with an African touch." Rooms start at $70 + tax and include hot shower, community kitchen, A/C and a pool. Laundry service is also available.

SUNSET REEF HOTEL (sunsetreefhotel.com) (640 0012) is beautifully located on the south end of the beach. All rooms have A/C, ocean view, hot shower in the $100 range, including breakfast. There is also a pool and a Jacuzzi -- great place to have a sunset cocktail.

VISTA DE OLAS (bungalows-vistadeolas.com) (640 0183) is located just up the hill from the main road. This small family-owned hotel has a wet bar, infinity pool and Jacuzzi with a fantastic view to the Malpaís and Santa Teresa area. Villas start at around $175 for 2 people including taxes and breakfast. It costs $10 for every extra person. Rooms have A/C, fan, hot shower, a fridge, coffee maker and a safe. They also have a great BBQ restaurant and deli with solid steaks and sandwiches. This is an ideal place to bring a girlfriend or family.

HOTEL LA HACIENDA (laciendademalpais.com) (640 0067) is a luxurious western-style hotel with an oasis-like pool and surroundings. Prices start at $130 + tax and include breakfast. They also have a nice restaurant open to the public.

Where to Munch
MALPAÍS SURF CAMP has a restaurant with surfer-friendly atmosphere and good drinks; a fun place to meet people.

MARY'S, on the south end of Malpaís, is a tasty and reliable dinner choice.

VISTA DE OLAS has a restaurant and a wet bar with a chef and a dreamed ocean view. Call them to find out about their afternoon BBQ's (640 0183). This is a place where you bring your better half for a romantic sunset.

WHY COME HERE The most beautiful beaches, offshore winds in the dry season, softer and more perfect waves, lots of sunshine, bikinis and fun night life; anything else?

BEST MONTHS
Dry Season: December to April, anytime there is a swell;
Wet Season: April to August in the mornings and evenings. September and October: Forget it!

BEST HOME BASES Tamarindo and Santa Teresa.

TRANSPORTATION Renting a car is highly recommended.

SURFING HIGHLIGHTS Potrero Grande, Roca Bruja, Playa Grande, Playa Negra, Santa Teresa.

MOST CROWDED Potrero Grande, Playa Grande, Playa Negra, Santa Teresa.

COSTS Renting a car is the most expense, but it is well worth it. Accommodations during Christmas, New Years and Easter can double in price.

DANGERS Dust, potholes, blistering sun, jellyfish, scorpions, mud pits and beautiful women!

BOARDS TO BRING Small wave boards, long boards and a small pintail for bigger swells.

DON'T FORGET Sunscreen, 2-2 mm wetsuit for Peña Bruja if you come December to April.

ALSO VISIT Volcán Arenal: September and October are best months.

DON'T MISS
The bull rodeos, Soda Las Palmas in Villarreal, Lola's in Avellanas, ceviche de cambute in Manzanillo, the mecanical bull at Malpaís Surf Camp.

Power...

Central Pacific Region

Photo: Shifi
Surfer: Chuky
Location: El Hoyo

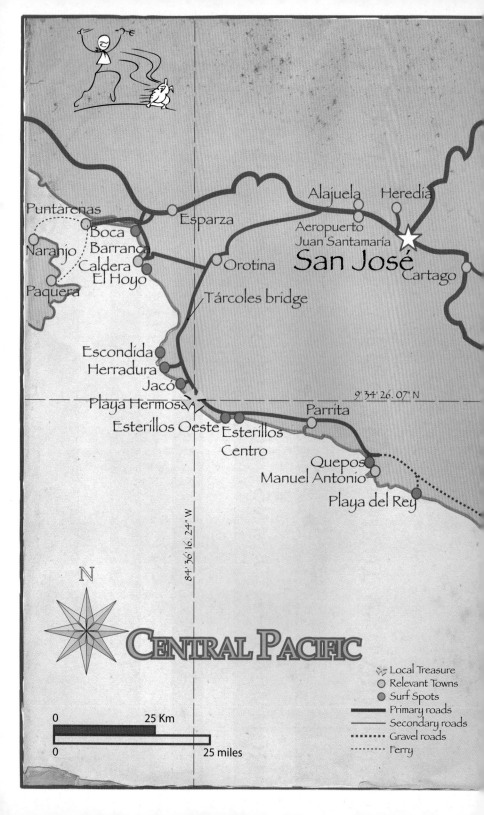

CENTRAL PACIFIC REGION

This is a lush area of the country, easily accessible and with consistent, powerful waves.

It is also the land for meeting crocodiles, poisonous snakes, brightly colored frogs, macaws and other various cuddly animals in their natural habitat.

Carara and Manuel Antonio national parks are both located in this region and hiking through them can be just as rewarding as getting shacked silly in Hermosa. Remember that you are in one of the world's most varied and densely populated (in terms of non-human species) wilderness areas.

The surf scene is quite wild as well. It's best characterized as having ruthless waves that break a lot of boards. This area is tube-rider heaven.

The rainy season is a good time for surfing the Central Pacific because the waves maintain good size and are often classically-shaped.

BOCA BARRANCA

The Surf

Boca Barranca is the second longest left in Costa Rica, beat only by Pavones. It requires a big south swell to break classic, although it is more open to the SW, and is worth checking on big SW swells.

The first section is nicknamed La Mariposa (The Butterfly) for its resemblance to a butterfly spreading its wings when the main peak unfolds. La Mariposa has a good barrel section at dead low tide when the size and right swell direction allow, but the rides get progressively fatter as they go along and as the tide rises. At high tide, the wave is mush. The water can be murky and nasty at times, especially in the months of May, September and October when it rains the most, but once you are there your opinion may be easily changed by neck pains from staring at the waves as they spin their long way through the horizon. Boca Barranca is an excellent longboard wave, but it is also fun for short-boarders because some sections are speedy and spontaneous. When the swell is small the sections do not connect, but the rides can still last. Going from the Central Pacific to the North Pacific or vice versa, Barranca is a good place to stop, stretch and check out the surf.

The Village

Boca Barranca started off as a weekend getaway for people from San José. Today the little village is mostly known for its surf.

Orly Apel

How to Get There

By car
The Barranca Bridge is 57 kilometers north of Jacó and not very far south of the intersection with the Pan-American Highway, the fastest way from San José. The path to the spot is about 100 meters north of the Barranca Bridge in front of Hotel Boca Barranca.

By bus
Buses run between Puntarenas and Quepos and pass the little town of Barranca a few times each day.

Where to Crash

HOTEL BOCA BARRANCA (663 6133). owned by Katia Arrieta, descended from the first generation to ever come to Boca Barranca, offers comfortable new rooms with semi-orthopedic beds, A/C, H/S, and TV in walking distance to the surf spot in the $50 range. Each room has space for up to 4 people, and she also serves great food.

SURF INN (663 81 55) is closest to the break and their rooms include A/C, TV, and as owner Hannia says, "a real breakfast. No American B.S.! I serve huge gallo pinto, scrambled eggs, ham, fresh fruit, coffee and bread." She also includes dinner and laundry service, all for $35 pp.

HOTEL RIO MAR, across the street from Hotel Boca Barranca, is not the best place to stay but it is close to the surf. Their rates go from $10 to $20 dollars pp, depending on the room.

HOTEL FIESTA, south of the break, is a good reference point. If you go from there to the road perpendicular to the main road, you will find a variety of places to stay in the next two kilometers.

CABINAS EL SUEÑO (663 4948) is a motel-style place with a Jacuzzi and A/C for about $25 per room.

CABINAS CASA CANADIENSE (663 0287) has a pool, equipped kitchen, and a green area with monkeys and birds for about $40 for 2 people; $10 more for every other person and extra for A/C.

VILLAS PALMAS DEL MAR (663 1736) is the best of a group of similar neighboring hotels. Their charming little bungalows have space for up to 8 people, their prices in the dry season average $15 to $35 pp and can drop down to half the price in the rainy season, which is when the waves are best. All rooms are fully equipped and include a pool and green areas right near the beach.

NOTE

If you plan to stay in Barranca over the weekend call as far in advance as possible to make a reservation as the places to stay fill up quickly due to its proximity to San José.

⫲ Where to Munch

RESTAURANTE LA CASA DEL MEDICO, 200 meters north of Hotel Fiesta has good seafood and a pool.

HOTEL BOCA BARRANCA serves cheap local meals for their guests and walk-ins.

EL VELERO DE MANUEL, parallel to Villas Palmas Del Mar, is where locals go to get drunk and eat seafood and bocas.

MARIA ISABEL ARIAS, the woman who lives on the corner of Surf Inn, always has ice-cold coconut milk in case you get thirsty.

There are also a couple of sodas on the way to Caldera.

EL HOYO

The Surf

This is one of the roundest and most ruthless waves in Costa Rica, and by far the best ride for sponges who charge. El Hoyo can be surfed all year round but SW swells are best, and it does not need a big swell to be on.

El Hoyo was peculiarly man-made, by accident, when the government built a pier to block the swells from coming into the Caldera Port, which harbors massive cargo ships. Back in the 1980s, two local boogie boarders from the area were walking back along the beach after being skunked at another spot. Their attention was drawn to what seemed like a hollow right spinning and spitting right next to the pier. They walked closer to make sure they were not seeing things, and Eureka! Their jaws dropped to the sand when they realized what they had found.

El Hoyo means "The Hole" in Spanish, so go figure.

At low tide, El Hoyo should only be antagonized by sponge riders willing to get bucked off and tossed around. The drops become more achievable for surfers after mid-tide when the drop is not as suicidal. When this place gets bigger than an 8 foot face, it reaches a new level of surfing that excludes all beginners and intermediate surfers without exceptions. Wipeouts can be violent and bloody.

On big swells, go up on the pier and walk to the end of it… have a look around, and see if there is something you like.

Note
A lot is said about heavy localism in El Hoyo. But just like any other spot where the waves can be harmful, you must show respect to the locals, and not paddle straight to the peak upon arrival. Stay in the channel for a while and wait for your turn. You will be treated with respect.

The Place

This is a spot located inside of a port next to a pier. You must park your wheels outside of the port and walk about 30 minutes to the break.

Photo: Shifi
Rider: Olger

Photo: Rodolfo Sommer

How to Get There

By car
The turn to the port is 6.5 kilometers south of Boca Barranca, though there are currently no road signs. The turn is the first main road, right after the Caldera bridge.

You have to park your car in the entrance to the port since private vehicles are not allowed inside, then walk about a mile to the beach following the path left of the main buildings.

Photo: Paco Salmeron

By boat
You can also negotiate a lift with the fishermen at the south end of the bridge in Caldera, ask for "Gallinita", he is a good man!

Where to Crash

CABINAS CALDERA right near the port, has decent rooms with A/C, TV, a pool, private parking and security for $30 for a double room. There is a seafood restaurant right next door. You can also stay in Boca Barranca.

Where to Munch

There is a local restaurant serving decent seafood next door to Cabinas Caldera on the north east side of the bridge.

Explore

El Hoyo was the unusual discovery of someone not looking for a new break. For those who look, there are other crazy spots somewhere near

there. Long walks along abandoned trails and cliffs full of poisonous snakes may be involved. During SW swells over 10 feet, it may be worth the hike… unless, of course, I am just playing. But if I were you, I would bring at least a friend and a pair of dippers.

TARCOLES RIVER STOP
There is a stop about 34 kilometers south of Boca Barranca that you don't want to miss. It is the Tarcoles River, where you can see huge crocodiles bathing under the blistering sun. Park your car in front of the restaurant, (leave absolutely nothing in, or on the car!) walk on the bridge and don't fall.

The best time to see these disturbing dinosaurs is during the dry season months. In the wet season they often get washed away to the sea…

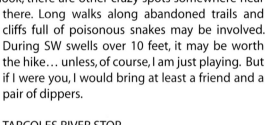

Got balls?

PLAYA ESCONDIDA

 ## The Surf

Just thinking about it makes my heart pump faster. This wave is simply incredible. The waves are juicy and hollow, the water is crystal clear and the take off is rough, but not criminal. Just about everybody who has had the pleasure of surfing this spot refers to it as a perfect point break.

Escondida is one of the best waves in the country and can hold a solid ten feet in the face before it starts to wall up and get out of control. Escondida is a great wave for maneuvers and barrels, especially in the left.

The lefts have better shape than the rights, but you can get barreled both ways. Escondida is not an everyday wave like Hermosa; it needs a fair amount of swell to break overhead. SW swells are good for it, and it holds similar shape whether it is 5 feet or 10.

This wave is best surfed at rising mid-tide when the wave unfolds at the right speed and maintains good shape. At dead low tide, when the waves break too fast and the reef goes nearly dry, it regularly eats people alive. Don't do it. The surrounding beach is spectacular and there are a lot of fish swimming around under you. Not spectacular at all is the crowd, which can be dense during the weekends and holidays when all the people who have houses in the private gated community in front of the break add to the people who come in by boat. Target weekdays in the early morning.

March and April are the beginning months for this wave.

The Place

Playa Escondida is a good-looking beach with a private access limited to the homeowners of a private gated community.

How to Get There
By boat
Playa Herradura is the departing point for Escondida and La Isla. To get to Herradura you can take a cab from Jacó. If you are driving, head 3 kilometers north of Jacó to the entrance of Playa Herradura and three kilometers west to the beach. The boat guys will be there early in the morning, prices are about $15 to $20 pp, and if the price of gas keeps going up, everything else will, including boat rides. Thanks, Bush!

ISLA HERRADURA

The Surf

This is a fun point break with great potential, but poor consistency. When you come into the beach in Playa Herradura you will see the island to your left in the distance. If the swell is big enough this wave rises in scale of difficulty and excellence. La Isla shares similar swell directions with Escondida but not quite the shape, nor the consistency. If you were to fuse Escondida and Boca Barranca, you would probably get a profile that fits the characteristics of this wave. The rides can be quite long, the waves have the push that point breaks have, and it can be hollow, but it is more for doing maneuvers and cut backs.

The Place

Isla Herradura is an island at the south end of Playa Herradura.

How to Get There

Once in Playa Herradura you can do the walk 20 minutes to the south end of the beach or take a quick boat right to the line up ($5 to $10). At high tide when the sand is covered, you have to go up on the rocks to get to the spot. That is also when the waves turn slow and fat.

Where to Crash

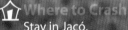

Stay in Jacó.

Where to Munch

There are a few restaurants right on the beach. Take your pick.

Surfer: Josymar Fuentes, professional surfer

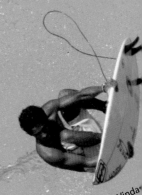

JACÓ

F-15 Fighter Jet Luis Vinda·
Costarican destroyer

SHIFI SURF SHOTS
PROFESSIO NAL PHOTOGR APHY
shifisurfshots@gmail.com
Phone: 365 4877

Surfer: Mauricio Umaña, surf instructor

PLAYA ESCONDIDA

HERMOSA

Surfer: Bruno Teixeira, shaper

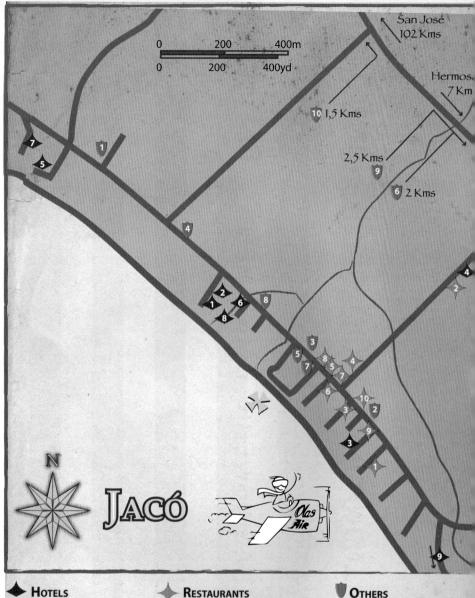

Jacó

JACÓ

The Surf

Just like any other surf spot on the face of the earth (including the ones in the Great Lakes) the waves in Jacó can be perfect. Yet on an average day they are no better than just fun. Especially when you consider that Hermosa and Escondida, two of the best waves in the whole country, are only minutes away.

During the dry season months, Jacó is the most favorable spot for learning how to surf in the area, due to its small waves that break on a sandy bottom. In the wet season months beginning in April, however, direct exposure to south swells make the spot a greater challenge for beginners who will face serious currents and bigger, heavier waves. A good clean SW swell at mid-tide rising in Jacó will make Playa Grande look like a harmless kitty cat. But unless high tide is in the morning and the swell is 6 to 8 feet it is not going to happen.

The best waves are perpendicular to Bohio Street, and in front of the Best Western Hotel. The crowd thins out towards both ends of the beach as the waves get smaller. Beware of strong currents.

The Town

Jacó is Surf City Costa Rica. Similar to Tamarindo, it is a fast growing beach settlement with plenty of entertainment, and the surf parallel to the main street. One remarkable difference: The Costa Rican population in Jacó is over 5,000; there is a real Costa Rican lifestyle than involves soccer fields, churches, schools, cantinas and a lot of local restaurants with great food and low prices. Jacó has a wide variety of surf shops. This is a good place to buy a surf board.

Jacó cleaned up?
Over the years in Jacó, there has been a dramatic change that involves a lot more investment and cheaper, better services. The town is a lot more hygienic than the sickening rat house it nearly became. Contributing reasons for the positive growth: the marina built in Herradura and the constant influx of surfers who keep the money flowing. But the increasing amount of "sea-men" flooding the streets of Jacó has also increased the number of prostitutes supplying the sexual demand. So Jacó is actually a cleaner town at the moment.

You like fish? Go to Jacó.

How to Get There
By bus
There are five daily buses from La Coca Cola Bus Station in San José and more buses are scheduled during holidays and weekends. Buy your ticket before departure as they sell quickly. The trip takes 3 hours and includes a stop for snacks, call 290 2922 for latest schedules. Coming from Tamarindo, take one of the buses that goes to San José (the earlier the better) and ask the driver to drop you off at El Cruce de Barranca, (ehl-croo-se--deh--bah-rahn-kah). There, catch any bus going south to Puntarenas and from there another bus to Jacó.

By car
From San José follow the road through Orotina (not through Esparza). Stop at the bridge over the Tarcoles River to check out the massive crocodiles.

🏠 Where to Crash
CABINAS RUTÁN (643 3328), north of the Monkey Bar has clean bunk beds, a fan and a locker for $10. Upscale rooms are also available at extra charge.

CABINAS SOL MARENA (643 1124), next door to Chuck's, is a family-run place with 8 cabinas starting at $10 pp. Rooms include private parking and a fan. A/C is available.

NATHON'S HOSTEL (nathonshostel.com) (3554359), on calle Central, caters "surfers, skaters and rocking rollers". They offer clean bunk beds in rooms with A/C, H/S and TV for $10 pp as well as cheap laundry service.

BLUE PALMS HOTEL (bphotel.net) (643 0099), next to Soda Garabito, has the best value in town with orthopedic beds, A/C, pool, H/S, TV, fridge and private parking starting at $30 + tax for a double room.

CLARITA'S (643 2615), at the north end of town, has decent rooms with TV, fridge, and a fan right on the beach starting at $35 per room in the high season; upscale is available. They also have a bar right on the beach where they televise sporting events.

HOTEL ROBLE MAR (643 2444) is conveniently located near the Monkey Bar in case you have to crawl home. Private parking, TV, and a small pool for $50 double rooms, and extra for A/C and a fridge.

HOTEL POCHOTE GRANDE (hotelpochotegrande.net) (643 3236) is one of the nicer and quieter hotels on the north end of town in the $70 range during high season. Their green areas are well maintained and they have a pool. A/C is extra.

CANCIONES DEL MAR HOTEL (cancionesdelmar.com) (643 3273), in the central area of town, is another good choice in the more up scale hotels. The pool is nice; the rooms are cozy and clean. Prices are in the $100 range.

HOTEL CLUB DEL MAR (clubdelmarcostarica.com)(643 3296) is the first hotel on the south side of the beach. The area they have is paradisiacal; a great place for bringing your better half (and let's admit it, you'll enjoy the luxury too).

‖ Where to Munch

SODA RÚSTICO, west of Pancho Villa, is where the locals eat. Flory Sandoval and Katia Salas serve the best local food, buffet style. The service is efficient and fast and the generous meals include a natural drink, all for less than $3.5

SODA GARABITO offers similar deals. The food is also tasty, plentiful, and cheap. They are located 500 meters east of Taco Bar.

PANCHI'S BAKERY has great pastries and good coffee. They open very early. This place is a local highlight.

EL BARCO The Italian ice cream place, just across the street from the bakery, has good home-made Italian ice cream for those hotter than hell days.

TACO BAR serves delicious fish tacos that include a giant salad buffet of over 20 exotic choices. All of the choices are prepared Mediterranean-style; clean and delicious. With huge one liter smoothies.

TSUNAMI sushi is a great place to dine, though a bit overpriced. The sushi, at least, is outstanding.

WISHBONE, owned by local surfer Caliche, is also a great choice for dinner and one of the most consistent businesses in town.

Other choices I like include Restaurante LOS AMIGOS, next door to Taco Bar; TABACON, across the street from Restaurante Colonial,;and EL POLLO PARRILLERO.

Ding Repair & Surf Gear
W.O.W (Walking On Water) Surf Shop (wowsurf.net) (643 3844) has the widest stock on clothing and surf accessories in the area, and quite possibly the whole country. Chuck, the owner, also offers ding repair, board rentals and a helpful surf report line.

Photo: Paco Salmeron

Photo: Melody

Photo: Paco Salmeron

WALTER SURF SHOP keeps a wide variety of surf boards to buy; anything from long boards to pintails at good prices. He does ding repair as well.

PIKO DISTRIBUTION (643 1121), owned and operated by Piko and Monge, has tons of boards for sell and trade. They also import top of the line surf boards and accessories. Piko is one of the main shapers in the country and Monge built a concrete half pipe in front of his house in case you want to stop by and break a couple of teeth.

EL PANA, on the main street, also has plenty to choose from, including body boarding equipment.

114

Night Life

Going out in Jacó can get crazy, especially from December through August, and on holidays and weekends. All you need to do is walk down the main street at night and find what best suits your taste; there is everything from stylish restaurants with fine dining to slimy bars full of sweaty prostitutes. Traditionally, the place to go out and meet normal people depends on the day of the week. Just ask the locals. The night usually starts at The Monkey Bar; Nacho Daddy's, Tabacon and Poseidon are also regular choices. Also, Pancho Villa is open 24 hours—fun, but a bit shady at late hours.

WARNING

There have been truckloads of visiting surfers who have fallen victim to corrupt police officers, clever prostitutes, car thieves and their own stupidity while trying to party like a rock star in Jacó. I advise you stay away from at least the most common scenarios that can cut your trip to Costa Rica short:
• Smoking marijuana or any other drug on the beach at night.
 • Driving under the influence.
 • Bringing prostitutes back to your hotel room.
 • Bar fights.

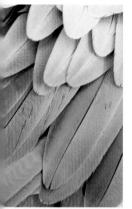

Medical Emergencies

EMERGENCIAS 2000 (643 2095 / 380 4125), found in the small shopping center located about one kilometer north of Jacó on the main road towards San José, is the town's most professional choice for the treatment of minor and major emergencies. They are available 24/7. There is also a public clinic at the south end of Jacó, but quite frankly I don't recommend it.

Tome chichi!!

Photo: Shifi

116

When the Surf Goes Flat

GO TO CARARA NATIONAL PARK This is a densely populated animal park. For those unable to go to the Osa Peninsula, this is a place where you can spot just as many animals in a wilderness setting. There are macaws, innocuous snakes, monkeys, and poisonous snakes and frogs (the ones you touch and die). The park is located on the main road, just 3 kilometers south of the Tarcoles Bridge and is best enjoyed with a guide.

HIRE A GUIDE Hiring a professional guide who surfs and who can take you anywhere in the country for bird and animal watching, or anything relating to a National Park, is an excellent choice when your time is limited. Call Randall Ortega Chaves at 643 1983 or 846 8621. Or, check out his web site www.costaricabirdingjourneys.org He speaks English, French and Japanese.

CENTRAL PACIFIC WAY (costaricaway.net) is a local travel magazine with excellent travel tips and recommendations for exploring round the Central Pacific Coast. Look for this magazine in the local shops and hotels in Jacó.

Local Shapers

You come to Costa Rica willing to buy a cheap board and sell it when you leave. Here is an idea. Get a local shaper to custom-shape the exact board you fancy, use it all you want and when you leave, sell it back to the shaper or a shop, and get more money back than you would for an average old piece of junk.

ALEJANDRO RAMÍREZ is one of the pioneers of surfing in Costa Rica and he has been shaping boards for over a decade. His label is his own nickname: PIKO. Piko works with his old friend (another Costa Rican surfing pioneer), ALEJANDRO "MONGE" CORDERO, in Piko Distribution (643 1121 / 643 4024) a shop they both put together a while back to shape boards, do ding repair and sell all kinds of surfing accessories and boards at good prices. Your board can be shaped and ready to go in 72 hours. Drop by their shop north of the gas station in Jacó and check it out yourself.

Surf Camp

If you are planning on coming to Costa Rica and staying at a surf camp check out www.wavescr.com, a small surf company run and operated by Andrea Diaz, Gilbert Brown and Nino Medrano, all former Costa Rican national surfing champions, who offer surf lessons and arrange week long trips in which accommodation, meals and transportation are included, on top of a daily session with the Pros. The goal to surfing with this group of champs is to better your surfing abilities whether you are a beginning rocky trying to catch your first waves or an advanced surfer seeking higher performance. They also have girls-only camps available and speak excellent English.

ROCA LOCA

The Surf

This is an excellent right-hander point break with stupendous performance. It needs a big SW swell to break. What it doesn't love is a surfer who backs off at the last second, intimidated by the giant rock that faces the take off. Then, the wave can turn violent.

Roca Loca is not very consistent, but when on, it is one of the best spots for bigger wave riders seeking an adrenaline rush. If Costa Rica were a giant bar and all the surf spots were different choices of booze, Roca Loca would be Grey Goose Vodka, just the right balance between strong and smooth. This place can get very big, reaching three times overhead or larger. Even then, it will still flow beautifully, as if it were only two feet tall. The best time to hit it is at dead low incoming tide, when the swells get a good grip on the reef. At high tide the waves get mushy and lose power.

This monster begins to awaken in March.

The Place

Roca Loca is a point break located at the bottom of a cliff between Jacó and Hermosa.

How to Get There

When you drive south from Jacó towards Hermosa, it will be at the top of the hill on the right hand side at the bottom of the cliff. You have to walk down the path (not really a path) by the almond tree, go down the side of the cliff and paddle out through the only water section in the reef right in front of the wave. It is not an easy paddle. Leave no valuables in your car, and don't paddle out if you are not sure about your abilities. The worst-case scenario here is ending up on top of the rocks, with big waves crashing on top of you.

Where to Crash

Jacó or Hermosa, whatever suits you better.

Where to Munch

There are no facilities in this place, but Soda Rústico in Jacó is just 4 minutes away.

PLAYA HERMOSA

The Surf

Terrazas

This wave is located at the very north end of the beach by the rocks in front of the hotel of the same name. The bottom is a mixture of rocks and sand. The main peak is a high performance right-hander with a juicy wall with tons of push, and a punchy lip that loops up very quickly. It is not an easy wave and it can be very cruel to innocent little boards. This break is best surfed during solid NW, SW swells at low rising tide. The rocks are sometimes exposed in the main peak's left-hander, but rarely represent a serious threat. The waves towards Hotel Fuego del Sol share similar velocity and violence.

Backyards

This is a mixture of A-frame peaks that break in front of all the accommodation places listed in this town's section. This is the least harsh section of the beach in Hermosa be-cause the waves break closest to shore and paddling out will not wear you out as much as paddling out in Tulin, for example. But, it will still tear you up. The waves are peaky, short and round making it the easiest place in Hermosa to get your pictures taken while riding a barrel (look for Shifi on the beach). There is a good right-hander in front of Rancho Grande that gets thick with big SW swells. This area is best surfed at mid-rising tides. It gets mushy at dead high tide unless it's big.

Surfer: Alexander Ramirez

El Almendro

These waves break in front of the big Almendro tree about a kilometer south of the Backyard Hotel. Very often you can see groups of scarlet ma-caws in the tree making a lot of noise. The waves break further out than in Backyard and are usually bigger as well. Right on take off, the walls start to spin upon themselves and line up nicely for a good 75 meters.

From the line up, you will often witness waves drawing Indonesian-like barrel shapes. This place gets really good when the swell is in the 7 to 10 foot range at mid-tide rising on a SW swell, but it gets extremely crowded on the weekends. If you park under the tree, DO NOT LEAVE ANYTHING IN YOUR CAR!

Photos: Shifi

 **La Curva**

The further south in Hermosa you go, the further out you have to paddle to the line up and the longer and bigger the waves can be. This is the case at La Curva, another one and a half kilometers south of El Almendro following the same dirt road. The spot is located on the corner in front of Piguino's house, a local who happens to own one of the coolest spots in Hermosa. You park in front of his house. The waves break far out but still on not very much water. I have been pinned to the bottom very violently here while expecting to land in deeper water. Was I ever wrong! Long rides full of barrel and maneuvering sections make it well worth it. This spot also breaks well at low-rising tides, hitting the jackpot at mid-tide and also getting mushy unless big on dead highs. There is better exposure to NW swells here than in front of the Back-yard Hotel.

Photos: Shifi

 Tulin

Bigger, longer, and thicker is better! Welcome to Tulin. This spot breaks in front of the abandoned houses a kilometer south of La Curva. During the wet season months this area usually is too nasty to swim in as it attracts all the trash that washes on to shore. If you ever louse something in Jacó's waters, you may find it in Tulin. But it is a whole different scenario in the dry season months when the water cleans out and the waves reach their best potential. And the potential of this spot is very high. At low tide, this place can flow like a point break and open wide like a heavy beach break. Good times when riding the long barreling waves, but good luck duck-diving while trying to get to the line up.

Tulin is a very demanding spot. If you are not in shape you may not want to antagonize it. February is a good month to be here.

122

Note One bad thing about Hermosa and the rest of the Central Pacific, for that matter, is that the wind usually comes onshore sometime between 9 and 11 am EVERY-DAY! So get up early for the morning tubes.

The Village

Playa Hermosa is an optimal place to drop anchor for a while, get your eight hours worth of sleep, eat like a horse and surf your brains out.

Extending for about 7 kilometers rich in terrific A-frame peaks, Playa Hermosa is a tiny surfer settlement with a soccer field and moody, lively beach break. Parrots, toucans and macaws are easily spotted towards the north end of the beach (the accommodation area), turtles nest towards the south end (Tulin), and punishing, spitting waves crash along the beach... the whole beach.

Playa Hermosa's long list of advantages include easy access, flexibility to break at most tides, year-round consistency, inexpensive food and accommodations with ocean view, peace and quiet, and literally kilometers of high performance waves.

But just like everything, it comes with a price. The violent nature of these waves in combination with its shallow sand bars does break hundreds of surf boards every year, and if you are up for the challenge, yours may be next. So bring a couple of boards, if you will, and tighten up your pants.

How to Get There

By bus

From La Coca Cola Station in San José catch one of the buses to Quepos and ask the driver to drop you off in Hermosa, or take one of the buses to Jacó at the same station and get a cab to Hermosa for under $10.

By car

Same as in Jacó but don't turn right into Jacó and rather keep driving south towards Manuel Antonio for about five minutes.

By donkey

Unfortunately, donkeys stopped carrying bananas, coffee and firewood on this road in the mid 1980's when they finally paved it. So, you are late for the last donkey. But if you are still willing to jump on one, check out your nearest tour operator in Jacó. I am sure someone will find one "EsPecial foR Yoo"!

Where to Crash

All of the following places to stay have ocean views.

RANCHO GRANDE (643 7023) has simple rooms (private or shared) with a fan, H/S, Com/Kit and pool table at $12 pp. Bryan, the owner, is a great host and has boards for rent.

BRISA DEL MAR (643 7076) offers clean rooms with A/C, H/S, TV, and Com/Kit at $15 pp. Denis, the owner, is a good tube rider and also rents boards, bicycles and even a car for a modest price.

OUT BACK (surfoutback.com) (643 7096) has new rooms with A/C, H/S, TV, and Com/Kit at $15 to $20 pp.

CABINAS ARENAS (643 7013) is a warm wooden complex with H/S and fan for $15 pp. You can also set up your tent in their front lawn facing the waves for $5.

OLA BONITA (olabonitacr.com) (643 7090) is owned and operated by Freddy and Johanna, two super-friendly Ticos who offer clean rooms with H/S, fridge, kitchen and a pool for $50 2p, $60 3p, and $80 4p.

CASA PURA VIDA (casapuravida.com) is a private house with a pool and comfortable rooms that include orthopedic beds, A/C, H/S, and TV, starting at $50 for two people.

Where to Munch

CABINAS LAS OLAS and BACKYARD HOTEL both have an open patio right on the beach where you can have breakfast while you look at the waves.

HOTEL VISTA HERMOSA serves a delicious and invigorating seafood soup and other inexpensive satisfying choices; very good, very cheap.

LOCAL FOOD is also found at the little soda with no sign, next door to Out Back .

BOCHA, south of the soccer field, has good Pizza and Argentinean empanadas.

JUNGLE SURF CAFÉ offers well-prepared meals that often make it the local favorite for dining out.

DON'T MISS
DONFOCARRON (whole fried fish), at Jamming Restaurant in front of Cabinas Arenas.

LADIES NIGHT on Friday nights at the Backyard Hotel; be there for good grooves and, drinks and of course, plenty of ladies.

Surf Photography
SHIFI SURF SHOTS
(shifisurfshots@gmail.com) (305 3432)
Hermosa is, to my taste one, of the most convenient places to surf in the country. Waves are consistent and break close to shore. To that you can add the bonus that Shifi, the most famous woman in Hermosa, is always there with her big hat, tripod and top of the line photo equipment to take sharp photos of you and your friends while riding spinning waves in Hermosa.

You can easily find her on the beach shooting early in the mornings or showing the photos in Cabinas las Olas during mid-mornings after the wind turns on shore.

Photo: Shifi
Surfer: Gilbert Brown (See cover)

ESTERILLOS OESTE

 **The Surf**

La Sirena

La Sirena is the spot right off the parking lot. It is a long and slow right hander that breaks on a rocky bottom. This is a good long board wave. High tide in the early mornings is the best time to be there.

Esterillos Oeste and Esterillos Centro are two nice beaches to go with or without waves, just for the sake of going to the beach and checking out something different. Stop by the bar on the beach and have a cold beer with a fresh ceviche.

The Village

Esterillos Oeste is a cool little beach town south of Hermosa. The beach is often compared with the beaches of the North Pacific region, because of the lighter colors of the sand and the water, but the waves have the power of the Central Pacific.

How to Get There

The first and main entrance to this spot is 15 kilometers south of Hermosa. The road is paved, so if you take a dirt road you are going somewhere else.

🏠 Where to Crash

HOTEL LA SIRENA (778 8020) is south of the supermarket. The quality of the service is not very consistent, but location is ideal and the rooms are pretty good. (Prices weren't available when I was there—don't ask me how that works exactly.)

RANCHO CORAL (778 8648) is a great choice in front of the beach with the hollow waves, their prices start in the $60 to $70 range.

🍴 Where to Munch

RESTAURANTE EL TROPEZÓN serves good local food; there is food available in Hotel La Sirena, and there is a little pizza place near the beach, too.

 LA FELICIDAD (Esterillos Centro)

The Surf

This wave is located in Esterillos Centro and named after Albergue La Felicidad, a small hotel located right in front of the spot. The waves, like most of the beach breaks in this region, are punchy and can be punishing. They are not as round as Hermosa.

Mid-rising tides in the early mornings are best for coming here but this spot does not hold big swells. Still, the beach is a lot nicer than Hermosa.

The Place

This beach located just south of Esterillos Oeste mainly has a few vacation houses and one hotel built on it.

How to Get There

The entrance to the beach is 3 kilometers south of the main entrance to Esterillos Oeste.

🏠 Where to Crash

ALBERGUE LA FELICIDAD (778 6824) is right on the break and so far the only place to stay. A double room with a fan starts at $50 and an extra $10 for another person. A/C is available at a higher fee as well.

🍴 Where to Munch

Check out Esterillos Oeste.

QUEPOS

The Surf

 El Estero de Quepos

This spot is located right in front and south of El Gran Escape restaurant. The wave here is extremely fickle, possibly the most fickle wave in the country worth surfing. But it is also eerily flawless. When a solid NW or SW swell hits the river mouth while the sand is well placed by the port, this left-hander spins with a grace matched only by Potrero Grande (Ollie's Point). The differences are that this wave is a left, can be three times as long and is hollower.

This spot usually breaks no more than five times a year. Since you may end up passing by Quepos sooner or later, however, keep in mind that within the disgusting water that flows out of the town's sewer system (as anti-hygienic as it gets), hides one of the most beautiful lefts in Costa Rica. It's just waiting for the right moment to rise from the dead.

The Town

Quepos is a fun town located about an hour south of Jacó and 15 minutes north of Manuel Antonio. Most mainstream tourism in Costa Rica

Photo: Paco Calmeron

will come to visit Manuel Antonio National Park, one of the most spectacular in the country. Quepos is where you can stay and eat without ending up broke. It's also a good party hub between Jacó and Dominical.

How to Get There
By bus
Buses leave from La Coca Cola Station in San José several times a day. However, since you can't make reservations, it is best if you buy the ticket ASAP: they sell very quickly. If possible, take the direct buses, they are more comfortable (chance of AC) and faster. There are at least four direct and slow buses departing from this station. The trip takes approximately four and a half hours and usually stops for snacks and restroom breaks.

By car
Keep driving about an hour south of Jacó on the main coast road.

By plane
Quepos has a local airport with direct daily flights from San José.

⌂ Where to Crash

HOTEL MELISSA (777 0025), located close to El Gran Escape, has clean rooms and a balcony overlooking the street. Rooms have P/B and cost around $12 pp.

HOTEL RAMUS (777 0245), next to a liquor store with the same name, has average inexpensive accommodation for around $10 pp.

HOTEL MAR Y LUNA (777 0394), by Hotel Ramus, has small rooms with a fan and shared or private bath for around $10 pp.

HOTEL MALINCHE (777 0093) has nicer rooms with a fan, P/B and TV for around $30 for two people and $50 with A/C.

⫴ Where to Munch

SODA EL JARDIN, by the bus station, is a popular local place with good and inexpensive food.

EL GRAN ESCAPE has traditionally been the best restaurant in town. They usually offer fresh tuna and seafood, as well as a big breakfast menu.

Don't Miss
ITALIAN ICE CREAM PLACE, next door to Restaurante Dos Locos, by the bus station. They serve the best ice cream on the whole Pacific Coast.

Night Life
The constant tourist flow and the solid local settlement make for good nightlife in Quepos and Manuel Antonio. As the choices for going out change daily, I recomend you ask, but the night life in this town is fun and that is a fact.

MANUEL ANTONIO

The surf

Playitas

To find Playitas, you go to the far north end of the main beach in Manuel Antonio. The waves break on different sections of lava rocks and occasionally make good punchy waves, certainly fun, but nothing worth including in your schedule if your choices are limited. But, if you happen to stop by, it is another option to get wet. Playitas needs a solid swell to break, with surf time during the wet season.

The Village

Manuel Antonio is a classic romantic beach with light-colored sand, bright water and a few shops and restaurants, sitting at the gates of one of the wildest national parks in the world.

Photo: Paco Salmeron

Waves? There are some very good fickle waves, but aside from Playitas, nothing I am allowed to let out of the bag. More than a surfer's heaven, Manuel Antonio is where you bring your loving better half for a treat. If you don't have one, it is also a good place to find him or her!

Photo: Paco Salmeron

How to Get There
By bus
Take the bus from the main bus station in Quepos, a 15-minute ride. You can also get a cab, or drive to the main soccer field in Quepos and follow the signs.

GRAB A CAB Some of the bus drivers don't allow boards... in that case you can share a cab for under $10.

 ## Where to Crash
ALBERGUE COSTA LINDA (777 0304), near the beach, is a real bargain with decent rooms with private and S/B at round $10 pp. They also have laundry service available.

Photo: Vili y Josema

CABINAS PISCIS (777 0046) is located just walking distance to the national park and has choices of rooms with S/B averaging $10 pp and more private rooms with P/B, H/S, and a fan from $45 to $60 for two to four people.

HOTEL COSTA VERDE (costaverde.com) (777 0584), on the east side of the road to the beach, has fantastic rooms with a terrace. Prices start at around $120 including taxes and accommodation for two people.

SI COMO NO (sicomono.com) (777 0777) is traditionally known for good service and excellent facilities. Rooms start at around $190 + taxes for doubles, including breakfast.

Where to Munch
SODAS
There is a soda on every corner as well as local ladies cooking food on the street. Fried chicken seems to be the local thing.

LA CANTINA, by Hotel Costa Verde, often has good live music, tasty shish kebabs and other delicious treats done on an open grill. The space consists of remodeled train wagons.

Another good choice is the place right across the street from the main bus stop where they serve awesome seafood soup and cheap sunset Margaritas.

Ding Repair & Surf Gear
KOBE SURF SHOP (surfschoolbylocals.com) (777 5070), one block east of the main bus stop in Manuel Antonio, has surfboards for sale, trade and rent. This shop also has surf accessories and ding repair service. Alex, one of the owners, is the one you should talk to for getting surf lessons from some of the best local surfers in town. You can also drop his name on the beach; he can hook you up with a good surf trip. He is a very cool dude, with plenty of connections.

When the Surf Goes Flat
HIKE MANUEL ANTONIO NATIONAL PARK This is one of the most beautiful parks in the country, containing hiking trails that give you a chance to see monkeys, iguanas, toucans, sloths, etc, in their natural habitat. The views from the mountain trails are spectacular.

PLAY SOCCER ON THE BEACH Every afternoon, as long as the tides allow, there are pick up games on the beach; everybody is welcome.

PLAYA DEL REY

The Surf

This is a classic beach break for this region of the country: consistent A-framing peaks that carry a lot of water and push. Very similar to Hermosa and even Dominical, except that it is off the normal surfer's route and is known for having crocodiles. This lonely beach sits near the middle of a bone-shaking dirt road and stopping here when you are trying to get somewhere seems to make no sense. Think again…

Rey means "king". I am not too sure if that refers to a surfer being the king of his own beach, or simply to the size of the crocks that frequent this area… Maybe that's up to the person's luck, but I can assure you that El Rey has waves that rule. But don't even think about walking unaware in the mangroves. You may just help build the reputation of the next King-Crock.

The Place

Playa del Rey is an abandoned beach between Quepos and Dominical. The road is in undesirable conditions.

How to Get There

From Quepos, head south towards Dominical. Some 20 minutes later you will come across a little village called Roncador, where there is a sign pointing to the beach. From there, I suggest you ask your way to the beach.

Photo: Paco Salmeron

Where to Crash

Camping to get the morning glass is not a bad idea, otherwise stay in Quepos or Dominical.

Where to Munch

There are a couple of grocery stores on the way. Make sure you bring water and snacks with you.

CENTRAL PACIFIC TRAVEL TIPS

WHY COME HERE Easy access and consistent heavy waves from hell.

BEST MONTHS April through October.

TRANSPORTATION Easily accessible by bus from San José. Car is not required.

HIGHLIGHTS Tubes, tubes and more tubes.

CROW FACTOR There are far more peaks than there are surfers.

BOARDS TO BRING Boards that don't break. Including a small pintail.

YOU MAY NEED Mosquito net, an umbrella and an extra board.

DON'T MISS Soda Rústico in Jacó, and the Tárcoles River stop.

DANGERS Giant crocodiles, mosquitoes, dengue fever, prostitutes, poisonous frogs, potholes; that kind of stuff.

Adventure...

South Pacific
Region

Photo: Lance Clinton, Caribbean boys
jumping nuts at Pavones bridge, Pavones.
Jumping off: Rodrigo Froilano

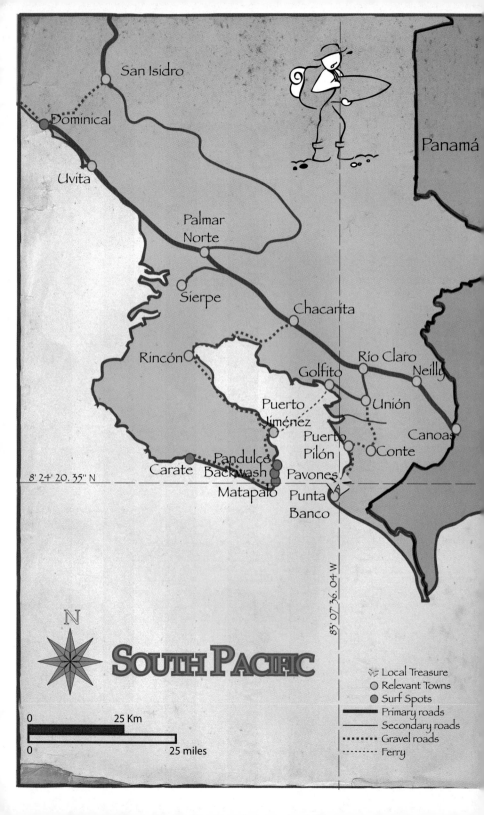

SOUTH PACIFIC REGION

Picture this: Let's say you find out about a distant destination with extremely fickle but long peeling waves and tropical jungle, deadly snakes, death-defying road conditions, poor medical care, isolation. Naturally, you want to go because you figure no one would make the effort to go that far.

So you take off on this mission to Surfer's Never Land, wondering if it is worth making such efforts, and when you get there after crossing mountains, rivers and sky, you realize that the place is as crowded as it can be. Now what?

A lot of people just like you actually are willing to make the effort of getting there to surf these famous waves, risking being skunked, dropped in on and humiliated by local punks. This is just the way it is in this region of the country. Travel time, distances and crowds can be inhospitable, but the waves and surroundings simply have no comparison. Frustration and victory go hand in hand in places like Pavones and Matapalo. Your final experience in such places (just like most places) depends on your own attitude.

Be respectful, patient and adventurous and hopefully nature shall respond the same way.

DOMINICAL

The Surf

"Heavy" is one of the most commonly used words by surfers who frequent this spot. I will add: hollow, juicy, consistent, fun and closeouts. Dominical's common denominator is its capability to produce billions of board- and heart-breaking waves any month of the year. It's always ready and keen to give you a taste of whatever it is you are looking for, including deep brown tubes and heavy wipeouts. Dominical gives the most size and push when the whole pacific side of Costa Rica is small. But it's also the first beach break to close out on a solid swell.

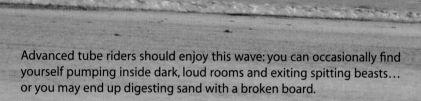

Advanced tube riders should enjoy this wave: you can occasionally find yourself pumping inside dark, loud rooms and exiting spitting beasts… or you may end up digesting sand with a broken board.

Hazards: Heavy currents and heavy waves.

Dominical is not a safe place to surf for beginners on their own; surf lessons are highly advised.

Highlights: The morning glass and mid-rising tide.

The Village

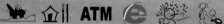 **ATM**

Dominical is a small surfer village located in a very green zone. The buildings are simple and not so numerous; and the beach somewhat attractive, but the mountainous surroundings, waterfalls, fun bars, and heavy waves make it a good fun trip.

How to Get There

By bus

Buses leave from the bus station in Quepos two or three times a day. It is best if you ask at the station. From San José you can catch the buses that go to Uvita from La Coca Cola Bus Station.

By car

From Quepos, it may take 45 minutes to an hour. The road is in tragic conditions. In the rainy months of September and October some sections are washed away. Then, you must drive to San José, and take the alternate road through San Isidro, or even better: Stay in Hermosa.

Photo: Ron Allan

141

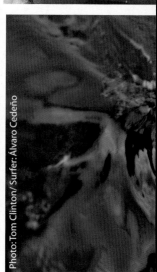

Photo: Henry Aguilera

Photo: Henry Aguilera

🏠 Where to Crash

EL COCO SUIZO (787 0235) located where the main street meets the beach, is a local place with simple rooms with S/B, and a fan for about $10, $12 and $15 for 1, 2 and 3 people. They also have 4 more rooms with ocean view, P/B, H/S and A/C for two to four people to share starting at $45. You can set your tent and use their facilities for $3 pp.

CAMPING ANTORCHAS (787 0307), right around the corner from Tortilla Flats, has a deck with a roof where you can rent a tent and a foam mattress for about $7 with access to electricity and a com/ kit. There are also rooms starting at $20 for 2 people with S/B.

DOMINICAL BACKPACKERS (787 0026), next door to Cabinas San Clemente on the beach, is a hostel-style place in front of the waves with dorms and a com/kit for $10 pp.

TORTILLA FLATS (Tortillaflatdsdominical.com) (787 0033) has rooms right in front of the peak with P/B, H/S starting at $30. Rooms with A/C are available at extra cost.

CABINAS SAN CLEMENTE (787 0026), just north of Tortilla Flats, is another good choice in front of the beach, with rooms with a P/B, and H/S ranging between $30 and $60 for two to four people.

SUN DANCER (787 0189) is not beach-front but has some of the best value in town with tidy rooms with P/B, H/S a pool and a bar. Prices start at $30 for 2 people and they have rooms for up to 5 people. A/C is also available at extra charge.

POSADA DEL SOL (787 0085) is a cozy hotel, owned by Doña Mariela and Doña Leticia, with clean rooms, orthopedic beds, P/B, H/S, and a fan starting at $35 for two people.

HOTEL DOMILOCOS (domilocos.com) (787 0244) is a hundred meters south of El Coco Suizo, with classic hotel rooms and a queen size bed, P/B, H/S and fan starting at $45 for two people.

VILLAS RIO MAR (villasriomar.com) (787 0252) is located about one kilometer east of the beach along the road that slides under the bridge. It is one of the nicest hotels in the area, with green gardens, a restaurant and a pool. Rooms here start at about $70 + tax.

‖ Where to Munch

SODA Y RESTAURANTE NANYOA is the cheap local place to eat. They have inexpensive meals and fruit for sale and are located in front of the hardware store.

EL COCO SUIZO is the other eatery in town. They specialize in seafood and usually have fresh ceviche and cold beer waiting for you.

TORTILLA FLATS, on the beach, has decent salads and sandwiches. Their main attractions are the view and a bar that appeals after a surf session.

RESTAURANTE SAN CLEMENTE, on the main street, has a Mexican-American menu with satisfying breakfasts and good burritos. Tuesday nights are "Taco Tuesdays".

RESTAURANTE WACHACHA is located around the corner from Tortilla Flats. It's owned by an Afro-Caribbean man, who translated any nostalgia for home into some amazing flavors. It makes dinner a good time to order any plate with seafood, spices and coconut!

RESTAURANTE CONFUSIONE, located within Hotel Domilocos, is a fine Italian restaurant with excellent food. This is the best restaurant in Dominical for a romantic good-tasting dinner.

Surf Photography

RANCHO TORTUGA PHOTOGRAPHY (Dominical.biz) (899 7785). You need to talk to Ron Allan McLean about this matter: "For your photos see me on the beach in the mornings or San Clemente Restaurant's upstairs internet café in the afternoons". He has a 20D with a good lens and usually shoots during morning glassy conditions.

Ding Repair & Surf Gear
PINEAPPLE SURF SHOP, next door to the Police Station, has the best stock of clothing, sandals and surfing accessories in town. They can also refer you to a good ding-repair man.

Night Life
Dominical is a very small place. If you saw someone you would like to meet again, chances are you will find them out at night. Thrusters is the popular local bar, but Tortilla Flats and San Clemente also attract a crowd depending on the day of the week and the time of night. Ask the locals where you should go on a given night.

When the Surf Goes Flat
DOMINICAL SURF & ADVENTURE (dominicalsurfadventures.com) (839 8542), next to the police station, is the most reliable source in the region for tours and information. Norma Pellot and Henry Aguilera run this Info/Adventure Center. They can direct you on some activities you can do on your own. Among these is a hike to Nauyaca Falls, a set of two giant waterfalls, one of which you can jump from (highly recommended!). HENRY is a local from this area who knows Costa Rica very well, is very profes-

sional and also surfs. Some of his top tours offer all-inclusive surf and adventure packages: he will pick you up and drop you off at the airport and take you surfing, rafting, rappelling, hiking, canyoning, bungee jumping and so on all over the country for a week. He can also put together a surf or rafting trip to any of the best spots in the country.

Feel free to drop by this place if you have any questions at all while in Dominical.

Medical Emergencies
CLINICA GONZALES ARELLANO (787 0129), located 100 meters east of Restaurante San Clemente, can take professional care of you as long as you get hurt during the day. Dial 911 if you get hurt at night.

OSA PENINSULA

The Surf

This is the richest place in Costa Rica for tropical jungle and animal sightings, and is included for that reason alone. The attraction of this area is its stunning natural beauty, not the surf. There are no regular surfing spots in the area. But, since it is directly exposed to the open ocean it usually has massive closeouts where you will be able to catch a super heavy screaming shoulder here and there. Definitely bring your board if you've come this far.

Note: Access to this area is very difficult during the raning season months.

How to Get There

By truck

The same trucks that take you to Matapalo from Jiménez also bring you this far. The trip can be a bit harsh so use a board bag if you bring a board.

By car

From Matapalo, continue driving on the road along the ocean. It may take you one and a half to two hours from Matapalo.

By plane

There is an airstrip by the Pulpería at the end of the road. You can charter a plane to take you there or fly to Jiménez and carry on by land.

Where to Crash

LA PULPERIA This world famous grocery store at the end of the road may have tents for rent for the night, but do not count on it. What you can count on is on their friendly owners having a decent stock of chips, chocolate bars and beer. What else could you possibly need?

LA LEONA LODGE (laleonalodge.com) (735 5705 / 735 5704) is a tent hotel located one and a half kilometers from the end of the road between Carate and the Corcovado National Park entrance. You must walk along the beach to get there. The set up is simple. You get a private little tent-bungalow on a hill in the middle of the jungle and in front of the ocean. Prices go from $60 pp including three meals and unlimited natural drinks.

Where to Munch

Take note that there are no regular places to eat in this area, so in case you come here and camp, make sure you bring enough supplies.

MATAPALO AREA

The Surf

Matapalo

Matapalo is a "male" version of Potrero Grande (Ollie's Point). It is bigger, stronger, faster (no offense ladies!) and can be far more uncivilized.

The wave is long and it breaks at a speed that seems to have no interruptions or disturbing accelerations. It just flows along, peeling along its shallow, rocky bottom like nothing else in the world matters. And, indeed, when you are surfing it, nothing in the world does. This wave is located in one of the most pristine natural oases in the world. The air here flows smoothly through the lungs, filling them with healthy, wholesome oxygen, as you glide along the water and scarlet macaws invade the sky.

Matapalo does not tube like Playa Negra, but it is longer and can produce wide, heavy caverns. More good things about Matapalo: It is very consistent compared to neighboring spots like Pavones. If there is a swell (8 feet + in any direction) Matapalo will break. It likes south swell more than west but attracts a lot of waves regardless.

Remoteness is another spice to add to the mix. There is no electricity, no water and getting there is a mission. If you are into roughing it and

Photo: Thornton / Surfer: Steve Petix

camping in a crazy place, in front of a sweet wave, you just found your heaven. Most negative aspect: The crowds, yes gods, the crowds! Oh, and don't forget the high amount of deadly snakes (and I do not mean it as a joke).

 ### Backwash (Mataplayos)

A speedy, peeling version of Matapalo. This peak usually breaks left and right, but the rights are better. When this place is solid overhead, the rides will be fast and tubular. Matapalo will be massive and scary then.

Lower tides are better for this break because the waves seem to get a better grip on the rocks underneath. High tide nearly makes the wave disappear. Tubes can be ridden on solid days in the last section of the rides. This is a very good wave. When you consider that, and the fact that there aren't that many choices in this area, you should understand why the place is usually crowded.

 ### Pan Dulce

Pan Dulce is the nicest beach in this area. You can often spot scarlet macaws feeding on the almond trees that hug the sand and white-faced monkeys chattering among the branches.

Pan Dulce is also the first break you come across after you take the path that leads to the beach, the softest of them all, and the best place to learn when the waves are small. There are a lot of rocks that expose at lower tides, so higher tides are better for surfing these soft, long waves.

148

When the waves are solid overhead in this break, Backwash will be bigger and Matapalo may be a maxed-out monstrosity.

Photo: Thornton

Backwash

The Place

Picture green mountains full of monkeys, birds and butterflies, stands of coconut trees and exotic surfing beaches, and add three simultaneous right-hand point breaks spinning merrily along: that's the Matapalo area. Matapalo is located on the south tip of the Osa Peninsula facing Pavones. Pan Dulce, one of the beaches, is easily the most attractive; dozens of scarlet macaws and monkeys are around throughout the day. From there, walking along the path towards the tip of the Peninsula, you will come across Backwash, then at last Matapalo, where the more serious waves are.

How to Get There

By truck

This is the local equivalent of a bus. There are local pick-up trucks with seats in the back that run between Jiménez and Carate several times a day. Ask at Cabinas La Esquina (735 5328) (The Corner Cabinas). Tell the driver to drop you off at the entrance to Matapalo and walk the rest of the way in.

By car

Follow the dirt road towards Carate from Puerto Jiménez. Matapalo is about 18 kilometers away. After you enter the first thicket of trees, you must cross a small, bumpy river. Take the first main trail on the left that leads to the ocean. This mile long path leads to several sections where the ocean is in sight. The first clearing is Pan Dulce, the one after the rocky creek crossing is Backwash and the end of the road is the beginning of Matapalo.

Where to Crash

CAMPING Matapalo is optimal for coming with a friend, setting up a campsite and surfing yourself stupid. This place is a true isolated, exotic jungle, and the surf is top-quality. The closest town is Jiménez, 30 minutes away by car (a lot more than that in September and October). In Matapalo, you stand at the gates of what National Geografic describes as the most biologically intense place on earth.

One thing though: You must come well-prepared as there is no water, no electricity and it rains a lot. So bring plenty of water and supplies. I would also recommend leaving all your valuables at a hotel in Puerto Jiménez (thievery isn't uncommon) and getting a plastic tarp at the hardware store in Jiménez to put over your tents.

CABINAS LA ESQUINA (735 5328), in Puerto Jiménez, rents out tents, foam-mattresses, camping stoves, pots and pans and can store your stuff while you are away.

ENCANTA LA VIDA (encantalavida.com) (735 5678) is one of the limited places to stay near the beach and has competitive prices for the area. Rooms are standard with a fan, not shabby at all, but the best deal here is the surroundings. Prices start at around $80 pp + taxes and include three meals.

STAY IN JIMÉNEZ You can also base your self in Jiménez and take one of the trucks with seats in the back that transports people back and forth to Matapalo. Make sure you buy the tickets in advance. The last truck leaves Matapalo at around 5 pm. After that you are jungle bait.

Where to Munch

Unless you are staying at one of the limited hotels in Matapalo, you will have no choice but to bring your own food and cook it yourself (refer to "How to Clim a Coconut Tree" at the end of the book in case you go hungry). Make sure you also bring a bag to carry all your trash out when you leave.

Night Life

As soon as the sun drops behind the horizon, the jungle in the Osa Peninsula is transformed: As the colorful macaws and toucans and the monkeys go to sleep, other groups of mysterious animals come out of the dark and take over the scene. In a matter of minutes you will realize that the habitat is completely taken over by a different crowd of birds, rodents and beasts.

Welcome to the local night-life! Try to stay off of the dinner menu.

Photo: Paco Salmeron

PUERTO JIMÉNEZ

The Surf
Puerto Jiménez has no surf worth mentioning, but the place can be a good home base.

The Town

Puerto Jiménez is the main village in this part of the Osa Península. There is a small airport and a few humble hotels. Many eco-tourists pass through here to visit Matapalo, Carate and Corcovado National Park.

How to Get There
By bus
Get a bus from San José or San Isidro to Golfito and from there board a ferry across into Puerto Jiménez. This is a full day (and maybe part of the morning and night) mission.

By car
From Dominical, you drive south towards the Panamanian border and turn right once you get to Chacarita. From there, the road is atrocious but the countryside is amazing (you should be used to this by now). Follow the signs to Puerto Jiménez. In a rental car it should take you no more than four hours from Dominical.

Photo: Thornton

By boat
Fast boats leave Golfito at 5:15 am and 2:00 pm from the main boat harbor. Reconfirm departure times with the locals when you get there.

By plane
There are daily flights to Puerto Jiménez from San Jose.

🏠 Where to Crash

CABINAS QUINTERO (735 5087) is the town's traditional budget accommodation place with basic rooms with a fan for around $5 pp.

CABINAS LA ESQUINA (The Corner) (735 5328) has clean rooms with comfy beds for under $10 pp for double occupancy rooms or inexpensive dorms with S/B and H/S. They organize public transportation to Matapalo. This would be my first choice for budget accommodation in town.

CABINAS THOMPSOM (735 5140), a couple of blocks from La Esquina, has basic accommodation with S/B for under $10 pp.

HOTEL AGUA LUNA (735 5393), by the boat harbor, has nice rooms with A/C, P/B, H/S, T/V and fridge from $35 to $70.

CABINAS BRISAS DEL MAR (735 5028), also located by the boat harbor, has newly remodeled rooms with A/C, P/B and H/S starting at around $35 for two people.

‖ Where to Munch

SODAS selling casados and empanadas can be found on almost every corner.

RESTAURANTE CAROLINA, on the main street, is the town's best restaurant, serving everything from veggie pasta to grilled fish fillet.

JUANITA'S is a Mexican place by the internet cafe (there is only one). This is a good setting for relaxing and gulping down a couple of margaritas.

PAVONES

The Surf

Pavones is the longest and one of the most phenomenal surf spots in Costa Rica. If you think that riding a wave the length of a whole football field would be fun, just imagine what it is to ride a wave the length of 10 football fields, non-stop with tubular sections and solid overhead walls to cut back and play at free will.

This wave is among the top on the continent… and of course, one of the most crowded as well. I have counted as many as 100 surfboards in the water with three to five waves that can be ridden at the same time. The only good thing about that is that you usually need only one wave to make your day. By the time you do the 25-minute walk back to the Cantina in front of the wave (where you can have a cold beer while you tell somebody about your good ride) you may well be a satisfied chap already.

154

eft on the planet

Photo: Itai Bar

One other good factor to keep crowd-whiny surfers from complaining is that Pavones can be surfed all day long, as both tides are viable and the wind does not affect the waves as much as it does in the rest of the country. You can easily catch one single wave in the morning, one in the afternoon and one in between and be a happy surfer who sleeps like a log (if you find a room!).

The bad news: Pavones is super-fickle. It needs a huge south swell to connect all sections and be classic. Also, bring booties if you have sensitive feet (wimp!); you will know why when you get there.

Internet swell forecasting has become an effective tool, to the point that there are people who fly in from other countries just to surf the swell and then go back.

Pavones gets big: two or three times overhead at times. And the bigger it is, the more perfect it gets. This wave is unbelievable. Generally speaking, Pavones is an incredible surf experience because of its exceptional long wave. However, I must stress the fact that it is crowded. I recommend you go elsewhere if crowds make you an angry, bitter surfer because that is just about the only sure thing you will find at Pavones. Dozens and dozens of us trying to catch one of the longest rides in the world, so… see you there (But hopefully not...Ha Ha!).

The Village

This is a very small, quiet village slowly adapting to its fate of hosting the second longest left on the globe. Getting here by car takes a long time and coming by bus is Mission Impossible 4 with you as the star and a

Photo: Rafael Garita

non-trendy soundtrack. When you see or ride the local bus, you will realize how far behind in time this place is.

Where to Crash

LA ESQUINA DEL MAR, most commonly known as "La Cantina", has three rooms that share a small shower and bathroom. One of the rooms has a direct view to the waves and usually costs about $10 pp for 3 people.

CABINAS MAUREEN, across the street from "La Cantina", has plain rooms with S/B, and a fan for about $10 pp.

CABINAS CELESTE has a few rooms in a wooden building for $10 pp. with S/B and two rooms with A/C starting at $40

CABINAS KAROL also has the classic set up of a simple room near the break with S/B and a com/kit for about $10 pp.

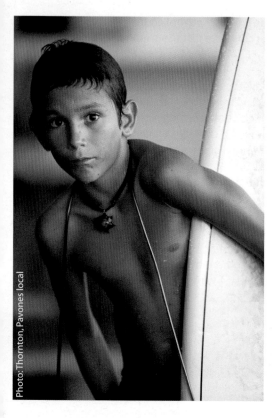

CABINAS WILLY WILLY'S behind Willy Willy's Grocery Store has three rooms with A/C, P/B starting at $40.

HOTEL LA PERLA, by Soda la Plaza, has some of the better rooms around with A/C, P/B, and H/S starting at $50 for two people.

PARAISO DEL SURF (394 9733), 100 meters east of Super Waves has 4 new cabinas with P/B, H/S and a fan for about $15 pp. Add $5 to $10 extra for A/C.

PAVONES RIVIERA (pavonesriviera.com) (823 5874), before the little bridge that leads towards Punta Banco, has three private bungalows with A/C, P/B, H/S a full kitchen, a safe and (as if that wasn't enough) cleaning service starting at $60 for two people and $15 for each extra person up to four.

Note

Every time the waves start, Pavones experiences a great deficit of rooms for people to stay. Show up at least two days before the swell so that you don't join the people sleeping inside their cars and under trees. Good luck with the crystal ball and the psychics!

‖ Where to Munch

SODA LA PLAZA (770 8221), by the soccer field, has for the longest time fed surfers with large and inexpensive meals. They also have the only public phone in the area.

PUESTA DEL SOL, on the south end of the soccer field, has satisfying meals and cold drinks and is located on the way to the paddling-out point.

LA CANTINA has a couple of local ladies cooking local fast food. They serve pretty good BBQ sandwiches and fries.

CAFÉ DE LA SUERTE, also by the soccer field, offers a vegetarian menu to soothe cravings for good food and something different at the same time.

LA MANTA (824 5047) has a restaurant that opens for dinner, serving hummus, shish kebabs, Thai-fusion food and other surprises. They usually exhibit surf photos in the evening when the waves are good during the day. They also have a room to rent and a massage service.

Ding Repair & Surf Gear

TURKEY TOWN, in front of the soccer field, is currently the only surf store around. They have all the basic surf needs, but bringing Sun Cure and maybe an extra leash with you is not a bad idea.

Boat Trips to Matapalo

Local fishermen take surfers across the gulf into Matapalo. Driving from Pavones to Matapalo takes at least four hours (one way); a boat will take 45 minutes.

A local guy known as "Machon" is the most popular boat man, but you can go south of La Cantina to the place where they sell fish and ask for Ulises Porras (394 9773), William Mata, Gerardo Lopez or Miguel Jiménez. Trips cost around $30 pp. They will take you there, wait four hours and bring you back.

When the Surf Goes Flat

GO FISHING The same guys who take surfers to Matapalo can take you fishing.

JUMP OFF THE BRIDGE The bridge is located on the main road on the way to Punta Banco; good fun! Make sure the river is deep enough.

BRING YOUR OWN ENTERTAINMENT Books, cards, Monopoly, tooth picks, you name it. Pavones is nearly flat a lot of the time and there is not a lot to do there.

Medical Emergencies

In case of a serious injury you will need to hire a car (locals will be very helpful in finding someone) and head to Golfito or Neily. The first place I recommend you start asking for help is Soda la Plaza, home of the only public telephone.

Both towns are about an hour away depending on road conditions. The nearby village of Comte also has a small public clinic capable of attending minor injuries.

SOUTH PACIFIC TRAVEL TIPS

WHY BOTHER Long phenomenal waves and jungle like surroundings.

BEST MONTHS April through August. October is too rainy.

BEST HOME BASES Dominical and Pavones.

TRANSPORTATION Very difficult; takes forever: renting a car is your best option.

HIGHLIGHTS Pavones and Matapalo are the best waves.

CROWD FACTOR Heaven or hell depending on your luck, but most likely hell.

BOARDS TO BRING Small wave board and a pintail for bigger days.

YOU MAY NEED a mosquito repellent, mosquito net, a tent, raincoat, ding repair kit, extra boards, wax, fins and leash, a book to read, a set of cards, and if you are a guy, bring a girl (there are plenty dudes there if you are a woman).

ALSO VISIT Carate and Corcovado National Park.

DON'T MISS Scarlet macaws and toucans flying all over the place.

AVOID getting eaten by a tiger (just kidding on that one... but not about the crocodiles)!

Survival...

Caribbean Side

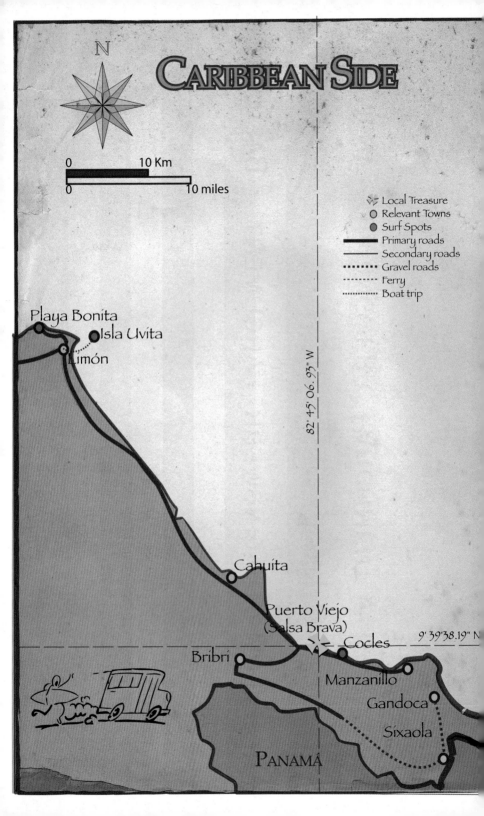

CARIBBEAN SIDE

Think of bright colors, Caribbean rhythms, Rasta vibes, dreadlocks, ganja, Bob Marley, Afro-Caribbean folks, coconut fish soup... it is all there. The east side of Costa Rica is a true Caribbean destination with an added bonus: waves; fickle, thick, dangerous, insane waves.

A lot of the inhabitants in this region are direct descendents of Afro-Caribbeans brought to work on a railroad that was used to transport goods from Limón to the Capital. Today, these groups have kept their own language, culture and traditions with an adopted Costa Rican twist.

The weather and the waves in this area are quite intense. Main spots like Salsa Brava are for experienced surfers who are willing to deal with competitive crowds and rough weather and surfing conditions.

Any time there are waves, they will be measured from the back, be intimidating, and be ridden by the top challengers who are totally freaking crazy!

Whether you are part of this challenge or not will usually depend on your abilities, your courage and, occasionally, your stupidity.

Note: Tides are not a major factor in the Caribbean.

PLAYA BONITA

The Surf

 Playa Bonita

This is a left-hander that breaks on a very shallow reef on the north end of the Playa Bonita. It's a Classic Caribbean style wave: a hollow, short, fast and dangerous screamer.

In the early nineties, a brutal earthquake lifted up the reef on parts of the Caribbean coastline of Costa Rica and, for better or worse, affected the performance of waves like Playa Bonita and Salsa Brava. It depends on your riding capability. The reef is undeniably higher, and the waves now don't need much push to hollow out and collapse. In fact, according to some locals, riding Bonita is like hopping on a set of stairs: you keep passing through a series of drops and double-ups that make the nearly dry caverns a dangerous place to be. There's a lot of adrenaline here when it's on.

Frequency: Not the highest, but not the poorest either. The months of December to April are the best time to check this place out.

 Los Tumbos

This is a surf spot created by the reef rising after the earthquake struck. Once upon a time, there was nothing here, but now a sand bar mixes up with some rocks and a hollow quick right-hander that loops like Terrazas in Hermosa.

A lot of boogie boarders and surfers who like hollow breaks come here for one of the Caribbean' most consistent waves.

Tubes, closeouts, board breaking, sand biting, everything is possible in this place, especially when it gets big, as it can hold solid swells. Go to the bar at Hotel Cocori and check it out: from there, you get an almost-above-the-wave view. This wave is not at the level of ferocity and quality of Salsa Brava but can sure make a random visit fun.

The Village

Playa Bonita is one of the beaches where locals spend family weekends and holidays. There are several bars and restaurants with magnificent views on the beach.

How to Get There

You can take a cab from the center of Limón to Playa Bonita for under $10 or you can take a bus from the main bus station in Limón for peanuts: just tell the person working at the ticket office that you are going to Playa Bonita. If you are driving, you must go through the center of Limón and follow the road north along the coast.

Where to Crash

CABINAS ROCA MAR (795 1504), on the hill across the street from the entrance to the beach, has simple clean rooms with TV, P/B and a bit of ocean view between $7 and $10 pp depending on the amount of people.

HOTEL COCORI (795 1670), literally right next to Los Tumbos, has the least friendly management I came across during my research, but also seem to have OK rooms and a restaurant with a great view.

Where to Munch

QUIMBAMBA BAR RESTAURANTE, on the north side of the beach, is a popular local hangout that serves meats, pastas and seafood.

REINA'S BAR RESTAURANTE, at the main entrance to the beach, has a similar menu and newer facilities overlooking the ocean.

HOTEL COCORI sits right next to Los Tumbos and it has a direct view to the tunnel of the reef across the bay. Great location for having a drink!

Ding Repair & Surf Gear

PLAYA BONITA WEAR (758 1642), in the center of Limón, is the only surf shop in the area. The owner, Yorgo Diaz, has a decent stock of surf gear and can help you with any questions you may have for surfing this area.

ISLA UVITA

The Place

Isla Uvita is an island a couple of kilometers out of the Main Port in Limón. Over five hundred years ago, Christopher Columbus came across this island (where the name Costa Rica, or, Rich-Coast originated) before ever setting foot on the continental mass of the country. It's a real shame the dirty bastard didn't surf.

The Surf

This island paradise has a world-class wave that wraps around a section of the reef that surrounds the island. The wave is juicy, island-style with a mellow drop and a fun wall to ride when it is head-high or smaller than ten feet in the face. When the swells rise, the waves adjust to the volume of water by producing obese lips that feed from the reef beneath before finding a way to move down the line. Basically, after this spot reaches ten solid feet in the face, it becomes a man-eating machine. This is no place to be if you like your body free of blood and lacerations. If, on the other hand, you are a pain-craving idiot who finds pleasure in riding mutant mobile bombs, come to Uvita on a big swell. This wave is not as rough as Salsa Brava but it tops the list of beautiful mutant waves of Costa Rica.

Photo: Walter "Teka" Fallas

How to Get There

WALTER FALLAS (758 1016), most commonly known as "Teka", has a couple of boats with solid motors on them, and he will drop you off and pick you up on the channel in Uvita. You just tell him what time you want him to pick you up and he will come back and get you.

To get to Teka's house grab a cab from Limón and show this to the driver: "Loco, lléveme a la choza de Teka, el mae de los botes en Barrio San Juan porfa! 150 Este y 25 Sur de la Escuela. Gracias, mi chiquito!" (The cab driver will know what to do).

If you are driving, go to the traffic lights where the roads to San Jose and Puerto Viejo meet and go to the next traffic light west of there. Turn left, then drive to the corner just past the school. Take a left, and go all the way to the end: you should be able to spot the boats.

Where to Crash

Camping is the only way to stay on the island. There is no water, electricity, or any kind of services so you must bring all your supplies with you. There are plenty of good spots to set up a tent. Keep in mind that it rains a lot here and come prepared to get wet.

Stay in Playa Bonita: you can take a bus or a cab from Bonita to Limón and take a taxi to Teka's house. He will have you surfing Uvita in no time. I wouldn't recommend staying in Limón.

‖ Where to Munch

There are no services on the island (that includes food and water!) so make sure you bring enough supplies if you are staying.

PLAYA NEGRA

The Surf

Playa Negra is the next beach north of Puerto Viejo. Not a lot is heard about this wave in the traveling surfer community of this country, but that does not mean it doesn't deserve attention.

Usually, when the swell is up in the Caribbean, surfers, a lot of them, gather in Salsa or Cocles to get their daily dose of waves. They build up a crowd that, just like any other crowd at a technical spot, can get a little hostile.

Choices? Hop on a bicycle (don't forget to bring a lock!) and head to Playa Negra. The best area is located towards the north side of the beach, at least some 15 minutes on the bike. Look for sections where rivers or creeks feed the sand bars. North swells are best.

Playa Negra is extremely fickle. But among all the choices offered this is potentially one of the best ones. What to expect if you score: Big round beach-break-shore-break beasts. Bring your spurs!

The Place

Playa Negra is a standard dark sand beach. Apart from its random good surf conditions and proximity to Puerto Viejo, it is not very attractive.

How to Get There

The best way to get there is to rent a bicycle in Puerto Viejo.

Where to Crash

Stay in Puerto Viejo.

‖ Where to Munch

There are a few places along the road, but the center of Puerto Viejo has more, and better, choices.

Photo: Shifi Etteinger

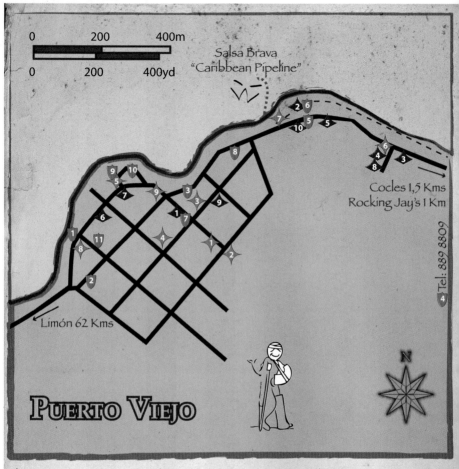

Salsa Brava
"Caribbean Pipeline"

Cocles 1,5 Kms
Rocking Jay's 1 Km

Tel: 889 8809

Limón 62 Kms

PUERTO VIEJO

N

◆ HOTELS

1 Hotel Puerto Viejo
2 Cut Back
3 Rocking Jay's
4 Cabinas Talamanca
5 Lizard King
6 Cabinas Maritza
7 Cabinas los Almendros
8 Bungalows Calalu
9 Casa Verde
10 Lotus Garden

◆ RESTAURANTS

1 Miss Sam
2 Soda Lidia
3 Café Rico
4 Bread & Chocolate
5 Pan Pay
6 Elena Brown
7 Rest. Salsa Brava
8 The Red Stripe
9 Dinner and a movie!

🛡 OTHERS

1 Bus stop
2 Banco Nacional
3 Frutería Yvon
4 Cariblanco Surf School
5 Caribbean Surf Shop
6 Ding repair
7 El Gallo Bicycles
8 El Gallo Scooters
9 Johnny's Place
10 Police station
11 Doctor

SALSA BRAVA

The Surf

Did you ever ask yourself why you surf?

It seems that the moment you picked up your first surfboard, life was either blessed or cursed to follow a path that involves a lot of traveling and never-ending new challenges. You always want to be a better surfer, catch a bigger wave, do a better turn, learn a new trick and on and on and on.

We all look forward to, sooner or later, riding tunneling waves in an exotic tropical place where exposure to danger and fear can produce enough adrenaline to make us explode with accomplishment and victory. Maybe that's why you picked up this book. "I should get this book," you might have thought back in paved suburbia, surfing two-foot slop in freezing water. "Maybe it can tell me where I can find those sick waves I hallucinate about occasionally." Bingo! Salsa Brava is one of those places.

As a result, I think you should stop whatever you are doing and get on a plane, bus or donkey and go straight to Salsa Brava, because it is probably going off right now!

One thing though: Salsa Brava is one of, if not the most, challenging, most technical, fastest and most dangerous waves you will encounter.

Photo: John Mathews
Surfer: Kemba

174

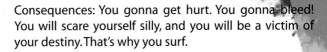

Consequences: You gonna get hurt. You gonna bleed! You will scare yourself silly, and you will be a victim of your destiny. That's why you surf.

All surfers who take on Salsa get hurt. Salsa is no regular surf spot. Advanced surfers or kamikazes only! This is the heaviest wave in Costa Rica; the Caribbean Pipeline. The set up is very simple: you jump off the reef into a freaky narrow channel and head to the peak. There you notice the insane way this wave jacks up and sucks below sea level.

The rights are longer than the lefts that don't always break. Bigger boards are recommended when the waves are over 10 feet in the face. This intense monster usually shows its teeth between December to April, but the consistency is quite poor so be prepared to wait.

The line-up in Salsa humbles most surfers who approach it (pros or not). So if sometime in the near future you see yourself scared to death in Salsa Brava wondering why the hell you do the things you do, don't be surprised.

The plain fact is that we are surfers and that is what we do (Salsa Brava breaks people and that is what it does).

The Town  ATM

Puerto Viejo has the immense honor of hosting Salsa Brava. It is also one of the coolest towns in the Caribbean side – it has colorful streets, tropical Rastafarian vibes, and of course, Salsa Brava.

Note
At the time of research and printing, various rumors about phone lines changing in the near future were floating around. By the time you read this, the numbers for this town may be outdated.

How to Get There
By bus

Buses leave from Gran Estación del Caribe in San José (257 8129) at 6:00, 10:00, 13:30 and 15:30. Call to confirm departure times, and make sure you get tickets to Puerto Viejo de Talamanca and NOT to Puerto Viejo de Sarapiqui.

By car
From San José, follow the highway through Guápiles rather than going through Turrialba.

By plane
You can fly into Limón from San José. From there, Puerto Viejo is only a 45 minute drive.

Photo: John Mathews

🔍 Where to Crash

HOTEL PUERTO VIEJO (750 0620), owned by Kurt Van Dyke (who happens to be a great host), is the town's most popular accommodation for surfers and young travelers in Puerto Viejo. Rooms with a fan and private or shared bath go from $5 to $10 pp. This place is just footsteps away from Salsa and the best local eateries in the village.

CUT BACK, south of Salsa Brava, is an original budget camp with plain rooms, tents S/B and a wood stove for all to share. Prices start at $5 pp.

CABINAS TALAMANCA (750 0425), by Elena Brown Restaurante, has plenty of low budget rooms ranking from doubles with a shared bath to private bungalows with a kitchen. Prices go from $10 to $15 pp.

ROCKING JAY'S (750 0657), on the road to Cocles, is the ultimate campsite in this area with tents, hammocks, shared rooms, private rooms and a tree house for, $6, $5, $7, $20 and $60 respectively.

LIZARD KING (750 0614), south of the break, is a well maintained guest house with a pool, a Mexican restaurant, and spotless rooms with P/B, H/S, for $35 for 1-3 people. There are also rooms for 4-5 people for $10 pp.

CABINAS MARITZA (750 0003), located half a block south of the bus stop, has rooms with A/C, P/B, H/S, for 2-4 people starting at $40.

CABINAS LOS ALMENDROS (750 0235), a couple of blocks south of the bus stop,

Salvador Van Dyke

Secuences by John Mathews
Surfer: Kurt Van Dyke
Note: All pictures did not fit!

4 5

10 12

"I grew up in the North Shore surfing Sunset beach and Pipeline, but I never got so many sick barrels put together, like I have at Salsa Brava"

- Kurt Van Dyke

.1 2a

Photo: John Mathews

offers new rooms with A/C, P/B, H/S, fridge, and TV for $60 for two people and $40 with a fan. There are also bungalows for up to six people with fully equipped kitchen starting at $70.

BUNGALOWS CALALU (bungalowscalalu.com), (750 0042) near Elena Brown Restaurant, is a small private hotel with a pool, a butterfly garden and cozy rooms with a fan P/B, H/S and cleaning lady. Prices average $15-$20 pp.

CABINAS CASA VERDE (cabinascasaverde.com) (750 0015), west and then south of Hotel Puerto Viejo, is a nicer hotel with a pool, Jacuzzi, excellent garden and poisonous frog nurseries. Prices go from $20-$35 pp depending on the room.

LOTUS GARDEN & JORDAN'S JACUZZI SUITS (750 0232), near Salsa on the road to road to Cocles, offers private rooms with A/C, king size bed, private Jacuzzi, P/B, H/S and an Asian restaurant with all you can eat sushi and a book exchange. Rooms go $60-$90.

🏠 Where to Munch

MISS SAM and SODA LIDIA are among the best sodas in town with inexpensive and generous servings.

CAFÉ RICO, just west and south of Hotel Puerto Viejo is best known for its great tasting coffee and breakfast specials.

180

BREAD & CHOCOLATE, west of Licorera Mane, is a very tasty breakfast stop with fresh bagels, fruit, and yogurt, among other choices.

PAN PAY south of the bus station, has freshly-baked goods and great coffee.

ELENA BROWN RESTAURANT, south of Lizard King, is THE Caribbean restaurant in Puerto Viejo. The food is always good and occasionally they have live calypso music.

SALSA BRAVA RESTAURANTE has an appetizing menu with a healthy fusion of Caribbean and Mediterranean food.

THE RED STRIPE, next door to the Sunset Bar, serves authentic and delicious Thai plates with flavors worthy of kings and queens. During the day, the owner usually keeps something interesting on the menu to snack or munch on.

Don't Miss
RONDON, every Sunday morning, at Elena Brown restaurant. Locals from all over the region suffering from a hangover will crawl out of their beds/graves craving this local delicacy. Rondon is a local seafood soup cooked with veggies and coconut milk, a classic of Caribbean cuisine.

Paaaati Paaaati! Pati is a local meat pie that makes a filling snack. You will see a local man with a hat on a bicycle selling this local marvel. His name is Pastor Franklin and he sells a very tasty Pati.

COCONUTS Some studies claim they are more nutritious than milk and have nearly no fat content. Fruteria Yvon (with a direct view to Salsa Brava) usually sells them nice and cold.

"Ceviche San Andres, se acuestan dos y se levantan tres". Look for this sign and try it out; this place has excellent ceviche and good food.

Surf Lessons
CARIBLANCO SURF SCHOOL (889 8809) "Monkey see Monkey do", is directed by Topo Hernandez, one of the most respected surfers of the Caribbean. He is the most reliable source in Puerto Viejo, has long boards and gives lessons where ever the waves are best for learning.

Bicycles and Scooters
EL GALLO (817 6533), owned by Jesus Gallo, offers bicycles and scooters for rent. This is the best way to get around in Puerto Viejo. Jesus and his wife Anita have a place next to Hotel Puerto Viejo and by Restaurante Stanford's. They offer excellent weekly rates.

Ding Repair & Surf Gear
SALSA BRAVA SURF SHOP (750 0661), located next door to Hotel Puerto Viejo, has all the basic surf needs and accessories.

CUT BACK usually keeps a ding repairman on duty, taking care of any board problems that Salsa is likely to cause.

TALK TO HERSHEL LEWIS (357 7703) Lessons; rent, buy and sell boards; you name it. Drop his name by the lifeguard tower in Cocles. He also does kayak surf trips. You will not believe what you are missing!

Medical Emergencies
DR. RODRIGO MARIN RODRIGUEZ (cell 831 4186) is a local doctor available for emergencies in the area. If you are not able to reach him, you can call the closest ambulance at 751 0008 or dial 911.

When the Surf Goes Flat
HECTOR JUNIOR UMAÑA PALMER (750 0306 / 824 4671) is a respected local Rastafarian. Nobody knows the Caribbean Coast, its secrets and its roots, better that he does. He takes people to national parks and arranges some of the most adventurous and culturally-dense trips in the area. From horseback riding to 16 other activities, he recommends:
- Gandoca-Manzanillo leatherback turtle nesting and nursery rooms (Mid Feb-mid July).
- Manzanillo wildlife refuge hike
- Gandoca Lagoon boat trip and organic farm
- Indian Reservation and Iguana Verde Project
- Cahuita hike, snorkel and cultural trip

JUNIOR is a very cool man and there is no better way to understand the history and the culture of this area than traveling with him. You can also contact him for long term accommodation.

CARIBBEAN WAY (costaricaway.net) is a free travel magazine distributed in all the main businesses in this area. This magazine can be a useful travel gadget for getting to know the area.

COCLES

 ### The Surf

This is the most commonly surfed place in the area when the waves are small. Depending on the positioning of the sand bars, this fun beach will have fast hollow spinners in front of the lifeguard tower or in front of the small island.

The waves here seem to get very square at times and break in shallow sections of water where currents build a sand bar. At times, this spot resembles a shore break in power and speed. With big stormy conditions, it is entirely out of control. Be there early in the morning to catch the morning glass.

The Village
 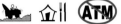

Cocles is a quiet village on a very colorful beach with a lot of coconut trees. The beach looks like a classic Caribbean getaway.

How to Get There
The beach in Cocles is a couple of kilometers south of Puerto Viejo. You can drive, take a bicycle on the main road or walk along the coolest shortcut that starts in front of Salsa Brava and continues all the way to the beach in Cocles through the coconut forest.

Where to Crash
CABINAS EL TESORO (750 0507), with a nice garden, offers shared dorm-style rooms for about $10 pp. They also have more private rooms with A/C, P/B, fridge and TV starting at $65.

LA ISLA INN(750 0109) has good rooms right in front of the surf. They include A/C, P/B, and H/S, TV and fridge and start at around $60.

Photo: John Mathews

TOTEM (totemsite.com) (750 0758) has nicely done rooms with a pool starting at around $70 + tax. Their rooms have a P/B, H/S and a balcony with ocean view.

LA COSTA DE PAPITO (lacostadepapito.com) (750 0080) has "Bungalows in the Caribbean for the noble savage." This small private resort has a spa and a beautiful garden. Their rustic comfy rooms start at $50 + tax for two people and may include two children for free up to 39 years old (seriously).

FINCA CHICA (fincachica.com) (750 0643) is the best deal for long-term accommodation as they have beautifully designed houses that are fully-equipped and located in a quiet area. The houses go from $50-$130 per day.
CARIBLUE BUNGALOWS (cariblue.com) (750 0518) is a high-end resort located on the road to Manzanillo. Rooms start at around $85 + tax for two people.

‖ Where to Munch
AGUA DULCE, just north of the lifeguard tower, has the most wonderful subs and smoothies in the region. They also rent boards and occasionally a room upstairs.

EL TESORO, found on the west side of the road before you get to Cocles, is a local style restaurant open for breakfast, lunch and dinner.

OTHER CARIBBEAN WAVES

Airport Rights

Tons of locals from Limón and Puerto Viejo describe perfect peeling beach break tubes in front of the airport near Limón, yet I have not found anybody who has surfed them and I am not so keen to start my-self, so I can't say they are good or not. The trouble is that the waves there seem to be fickle and the water is very murky and mysterious. Sharks? That's what everyone says, but who really knows ... The whole area from Limón to Puerto Viejo has numerous beach breaks that offer great surfing potential but need to be explored more closely.

Long Shoal

This is an outer reef that breaks about two miles or more outside of Salsa Brava. This wave is not very consistent but is gig, tow-in material for sure. Long Shoal is no regular spot where you take a boat to, this is more like a massive bomb that a regular surfer of Mavericks or a crazy Hawaiian nut with nothing better to do would love. This outer reef is not as heavy as Salsa Brava in its proportion but it is giant and heavy enough to drown a man without really trying. Long Shoal is the wave of the future.

Little Shoal

This is another outer reef that breaks south of the lifeguard tower in Cocles. The paddle out to this spot may take some 35 minutes or more depending on the inside conditions in Cocles. The paddle can get so rough here that people simply quit and go back to the beach.

Little shoal is a massive juicy wall with a lot of push and a long ride. After the odd section where the wave seems to vanish, you must be able to hook yourself into the next section. This wave can be very big and it moves a lot of water. Come here only if you have experience surfing outer reefs.

The Box

This Thing can't be described as a surf spot because it is mostly just a freak. If you walk some 15 minutes south of the lifeguard tower in Cocles on a solid swell you may be able to spot a couple of outer reefs out in the distance: the one to the left is Little Shoal and the one towards the south is The Box.

This place has nearly zero feet in the back when it sucks a few feet of water under sea level, before it begins to double or triple in size and acquire all kinds of vulgar shapes. When the impolite lips begin to land and produce loud explosions, this wave becomes a square mutant room that pukes its guts out. The Box has been antagonized by local chargers and they have brought tragic stories that confirm that this place is not a surf spot. It is a freak!

WHY COME HERE Rastafarian vibes, mutant-heavy waves, inexpensive food and accommodation, exotic and lively flora and fauna.

BEST MONTHS The main season is December through March with a short mid-season in June and July.

BEST HOMEBASE Puerto Viejo de Talamanca.

TRANSPORTATION A car is nice to have but not necessary. Rent a bicycle at Gallo's place when you get there and you will be set.

SURFING HIGHLIGHTS Isla Uvita, Salsa Brava.

CROWD FACTOR The main breaks are crowded with local high performers. Drop in on anybody and you are out! So remember your manners!

COSTS This is the least expensive region of the country.

BOARDS TO BRING A normal small wave board, a pin tail and a top gun with plenty of extra inches.

DON'T FORGET First aid kit, your top gun, a lighter, your Visa card (Master card is not accepted in the local bank), mosquito repellent, a lock, a raincoat or umbrella and plenty of balls! (And I am not talking about volley ball!).

ALSO VISIT Cahuita and Manzanillo.

DON'T MISS Rondon at Elena Brown Restaurante; renting a bicycle.

DANGERS Sharp corals, violent waves, falling coconuts, dengue fever, hangovers ... Thievery can be a problem too, so stay alert!

SPANISH SECTION

Same Sound & Meaning

Munchies
Leash
Bar
Track top
Pro
Cook
Surf Shop
Shaper
Shorts
Gay
On-shore
Off-shore
All surf tricks

Body Parts

Head = *Cabeza* (kah-**beh**-sah)
Eyes = *Ojos* (**oh**-hoes)
Nose = *Nariz* (na**h-ris**)
Ears = *Orejas* (oh-**reh**-has)
Mouth = *Boca* (**boh**-kah)
Lips = *Labios* (**lah**-beeohs)
Neck = *Nuca* (**noo**-kah)
Chest, breast = *Pecho* (**peh**-choh)
Back = *Espalda* (es-**pahl**-dah)
Stomach = *Estomago* (es-**toh**-mah-goh)
Hips = *Caderas* (kah-**deh**-ras)
Legs = *Piernas* (**pee-ehr**-nahs)
Feet = *Pies* (**pee**-ehs)
Arms = *Brazos* (**bra**-sohs)
Hands = *Manos* (**mah**-nohs)
Fingers = *Dedos* (**deh**-dohs)

Colors

Black = *Negro* (**neh**-groh)
White = *Blanco* (**blahn**-koh)
Blue = *Azul* (ah-**sool**)
Red = *Rojo* (**roh**-hoh)
Green =*Verde* (**behr**-deh)
Orange = *Naranja* (nah-**rahn**-hah)
Yellow = *Amarillo* (ah-mah-**ree**-joo)
Brown = *Café* (cah-**feh**)
Pink = *Rosado* (roh-**sah**-doh)

Numbers

One = *Uno* (**ooh**-noh)
Two = *Dos* (**dohs**)
Three = *Tres* (**trehs**)
Four = *Cuatro* (**kooah**-troh)
Five = *Cinco* (**seen**-koh)
Six = *Seis* (seh-eehs)
Seven = *Siete* (**see-eh**-teh)
Eight = *Ocho* (**oh**-choh)
Nine = Nueve (**noo-eh**-beh)
Ten = *Diez* (**dee-ehs**)
Eleven = *Once* (**ohn**-seh)
Twelve = *Doce* (**doh**-seh)
Thirteen = *Trece* (**treh**-seh)
Fourteen = *Catorce* (kah-**tohr**-she)
Fifteen = *Quince* (**keen**-seh)
Sixteen = *Diez y seis*
        (dee-ehs-ee-**seh-ees**)
Twenty = *Veinte* (**beh-een**-teh)
Twenty one = *Veintiuno*
        (beh-een-**tee-oo**-noh)
Twenty two = *Veintidós* (beh-een-tee-**dos**)
Thirty = *Treinta* (**treh-inn**-tah)
Thirty one = *Treinta y uno* (tren-inn-tah-**ee-oo**-noh)
Fourty = *Cuarenta* (koo-ah-**rehn**-tah)
Fourty one = *Cuarenta y uno* (koo-ah-rehn-tah-**ee-oo**-noh)
Fifty = *Cincuenta* (seen-**koo-ehn**-tah)

Sixto = *Sesenta* (seh-**sehn**-tah)
Seventy = *Setenta* (seh-**tehn**-tah)
Eighty = *Ochenta* (oh-**zch-en**-tah)
Ninety = *Noventa* (noh-**behn**-tah)
One hundred = *Cien* (**see-ehn**)

Directions
Right = *Derecha* (deh-**reh**-chah)
Left = *Izquierda* (ees-**kee-ehr**-dah)
Up = *Arriba* (ah-**ree**-bah)
Down = *Abajo* (ah-**bah**-ho)
North = *Norte* (**nohr**-teh)
South = *Sur* (**soor**)
East = *Este* (**ehs**-teh)
West = *Oeste* (oh-**ehs**-teh)
Behind = *Atrás* (ah-**trahs**)
Forward = *Adelante* (ah-deh-**lahn**-teh)

Food
Food = *Comida* (coh-**mee**-dah)
Spoon = *Cuchara* (koo-**zchah**-rah)
Fork = *Tenedor* (teh-neh-**dohr**)
Knife = *Cuchillo* (koo-**zchee**-joh)
Breakfast = *Desayuno* (dehs-ah-**joo**-noh)
Lunch = *Almuerzo* (ahl-**moo-ehr**-soh)
Dinner = *Cena* (**seh**-nah)
Beer = *Cerveza* (cehr-**beh**-sah)
Rice = *Arroz* (ah-**rohs**)
Beans = *Frijoles* (free-**hoh**-lehs)
Salad = *Ensalada* (ehn-sah-**lah**-dah)
Fruit = *Frutas* (**froo**-tahs)
Shakes = *Batidos* (bah-**tee**-dohs)
Vegetables = *Verduras* (behr-**doo**-rahs)
Meat = *Carne* (**cahr**-neh)
Seafood = *Mariscos* (mah-**rees**-kos)
Starters = *Entradas* (ehn-**trah**-dah)
Dessert = *Postres* (**pos**-trehs)

Surf Terms
Wave = *Ola* (**oh**-lah)
Surf board = *Tabla* (**tah**-blah)
Wax = *Cera* (**seh**-rah)
Surfer = *Surfo* (**soor**-foh)
Board shorts = *Panta* (**pahn**-tah)

Tubes = *Tubos* (**two**-bohs)

Others
Bicycle = *Bicicleta* (bee-see-**kleh**-tah)
Motorcycle = *Moto* (**moh**-toh)
Weed = *Mota* (**moh**-tah)
Car = *Carro* (**cah**-roh)
Friend = *Amigo* (ah-**mee**-goh)
Girlfriend = *Novia* (**noh**-beeah)
Boyfriend = *Novio* (**noh**-beeoh)

Verbs
To wake up = *Despertar*
    (dehs-pehr-**tahr**)
To stretch = *Estirar* (ehs-tee-**rahr**)
To eat = *Comer* (coh-**mehr**)
To drive = *Manejar* (mah-neh-**hahr**)
To surf = *Surfear* (soor-**feh-ahr**)
To go out = *Salir* (sah-**leer**)
To party = *Enfiestarse*
    (ehn-fee-ehs-**tahr**-seh)
To drink = *Tomar* (toh-**mahr**)
To hunt = *Cazar* (kah-**sahr**)
To flirt = *coquetear*
    (koh-keh-**teh-ahr**)
To sleep = *Dormir* (dohr-**meer**)
To snore = *Roncar* (rohn-**kahr**)

Manners
Please = *Por favor* (pohr-pha-**bohr**)
Thank you = *Gracias* (**gras**sy-ass)
No thank you = *No gracias*
    (**noh-gras**sy-ass)
My pleasure = *Es un placer* (ehs-oon-**plah**-sehr)

Common Phrases
Hi! = *Hola!*
Good morning! = *¡Buenos días!*
Good afternoon! = *¡Buenas tardes!*
Good night! = *!Buenas noches!*
Very Cool! = *¡Que buena nota!*
Very Cool! = *¡Que Tuanis!*
I like it! = *¡Me gusta!*

Excellent! = *¡Excelente!*
The check, please = *La cuenta, por favor*

What's your name? = *¿Cómo te llamas?*
Where are you from? = *¿De dónde eres?*
How old are you? = *¿Cuántos años tienes?*
Where do you live? = *¿Dónde Vives?*
Do you have a boy (girl) friend? = *¿Tienes novio(a)?*

Slang
Dude = *Mae* (**mah**-eh)
Cool = *Tuanis* (**too-ah**-knees)
Buddy = *Compita* (com-**pee**-tah)
Guy = *Cabro* (**cah**-broh)
Girl = *Cabra* (**cah**-brah)
Chick = *Guila* (**wee**-lah)
Beer = *Águila, birra, una fria*
What do you want? = *¿Que es la vara?* (**keh**-ehs-lah-**bah**-rah)
Smarten up! = *¡Despabílese!* (des-pah-**bee**-leh-seh)
Cop = *Tombo* (**tom**-boh)
Penis = *Banano* (bah-**nah**-noh)
Vagina = *Empanada* (emp-pah-**nah**-dah)

What to Bring
Support the local economy; you can get just about anything you need in Costa Rica. But there are some things you should bring with you, like a pocket size Spanish-English dictionary or a phrase book, good zinc oxide, a 2MM (if you are going to Peña Bruja between December and April), lots of stickers (to give away), power bars (not to give away), a good towel, Swiss Army knife, a small Mag Lite, music and board straps.

For anything else, as long as you have a finger to point and money in your pocket, you will be set to go!

¡El menú, por favor!

Costa Rica is a young country with fertile land and a practical eating culture. Our normal lunch menu, nicknamed "casado", is a huge plate of rice and beans, mixed vegetables, salad, sweet plantain, and grilled fish, chicken, pork or beef that is served with a natural fruit drink such as tamarind, pineapple, mango, or watermelon – a great meal when you are surfed out and hungry.

"Gallo pinto", the most common breakfast choice, is rice and beans mixed together and spiced with onions, garlic, cilantro and bell peppers. It is served with scrambled eggs, a corn tortilla, and coffee.

Also, each region of the country boasts its own local delicacies that have been cooked traditionally for generations. Tamales, chorreadas, rosquillas, tanelas, and buñuelos are some corned based goodies found in the northern region of Tamarindo, for example. However, traditional food is not usually found in local restaurants, and so it is best to go to traditional fiestas like bull rodeos or local soccer games to try it. There you will experience the whole package and even more cultural differences that you can test drive yourself.

The bottom line is: we don't grill, bake or deep fry cats, dogs, bugs or tourists (unless we get pissed off!), but from personal experience over the course of a lifetime, I can assure you that Costa Rican food and hungry surfers get along beautifully.

Pura Vida?

Pura vida (**pooh**-rah--**bee**-dah) means Pure Life. This is a local Costa Rican saying; a national emblem. Used very often, pura vida is a greeting, a way of saying "I am doing well" or "Life is good;" it is a way of expressing your gratitude and a way to communicate with someone you know

or someone you like. It is also a way of saying "hi!" as well as "good bye."
And, last but not least, it can be a sarcastic way of talking to someone
you despise.

In the surfing world it is often recommended by surfers with poor Spanish skills to others with no Spanish at all, as a way of apologizing when
messing up on the line up. This is not a bad way to use it, if you want
to sound like a dumb tourist. As far as surfing goes, keep the good old
"pura vida" strictly for greetings and socializing. And, in case you do piss
off a local and feel you must apologize, use: Disculpe mae (dees-cool-
peh—mah-eh), which means, "Excuse me, dude!"

Localism
Traveling surfers who have experienced Hawaii, California, Mexico and
other surf destinations around the globe can testify: Costa Rica has one
of the least confrontational line-ups in the world.

But, ironically, aside from our usual uncivilized local punks (me included),
there are also plenty of confused confrontational tourists who "localize"
certain spots like Playa Grande, Guiones, Matapalo, etc, because they
have lived there for a long time.

My only comment to that is: In Costa Rica, only Costa Ricans are locals,
period (¡…y nada de caritas!).

Hint: Local surfers don't usually speak with an Italian accent, or seem unable to speak Spanish. Heavy localism is not a major issue in Costa Rica,
but as surfers we should understand the rules of our own game. One of
them being: you respect the locals or you do not get respect back. I'd
like to think that if it ever came down to whom or what decides who
stays and who leaves the line up, it would have to be the waves and the
natural selection of the one who rides the biggest tubes. So, get barreled
or go home!

!Voy Mae! !Voy!
If you get to surf a spot with a big local crowd you may hear a lot of pe-
culiar noises and not understand what is going on. Most of the scream-
ing will probably be irrelevant, but if you hear loud noises like "Voy Mae!
Voy!" ("I'm going dude, I'm going! "), as you are paddling for a wave, it
means a local in the inside just claimed a wave and he or she is getting it.
Also, if you get to hear a loud "Déle, Mae, déle" it means Go, Dude! Go!
So: GO!

192

Skate Parks in Costa Rica

TAMARINDO SKATE BOWL: This is a concrete-snake shaped bowl, with intermediate and advanced bowls, located behind Hightide Surf Shop. Entrance is free.

MONGE'S HALF PIPE: Located in front of Piko Distribution in Jacó. This is an eight foot tall concrete half pipe with a short transition. Monge asks for a donation to keep the pipe well maintained.

JUNGLE GYM FLAMINGO: Located in the Jungle Gym on the way to Playa Flamingo. This is a square shaped flat transition with a couple of ramps and good rails.

ARENAS SKATE PARK: Located in San Pedro, San José, it's a good park with ramps, rails and bowls. There is an entrance fee for this park.

HOTEL TILAGUA: Apparently this is the best skate park in the country. Located in Hotel Tilagua (695 5050), on the way to Fortuna, eight kilometers from Tilarán, it is known for its excellent design for street and skate park skating and its magnificent view of Arenal Volcano. There is a small entrance fee.

ROAD TIPS

At the Supermarket
There are a couple of things you can always count on when you visit a supermarket in Costa Rica.

TRITS (treats) Vanilla flavored ice cream sandwich with crispy cookie-buns and chocolate chips... Hallelujah!

KRUNCHY Ice cream cone with a peanut topping. In case Trits are gone! MMM..io Chocolate, caramel and peanut bar with ice cream inside... in case Krunchys are gone!

YUQUITAS (u-key-tahs) The best chips, period.
PLATANITOS (plah-tah-knee-toes) Sweet plantains cut thin and deep fried; second best chip!

BIOLAND PRODUCTS This Company makes high quality organic products like Aloe Vera Gels, Cucumber Moisturizers and granola bars. You can find their stuff at most supermarkets.

Tipping at Restaurants
In Costa Rica, by law, 10 percent of your bill should be added as a service charge. Most of the better restaurants will also add 13 percent sales tax if it is not included in the menu price.

The 10 percent is usually distributed by the owner of the restaurant to the entire restaurant staff, so your actual waiter only gets a small portion of it. So, if they provided you with good service, they do indeed expect a tip. An extra ten percent is plenty.

Lonely Planet claims that "tipping above the included amount is unnecessary." Obviously their writers never had to make a living off of $1.05 an hour waiting tables like I have. I can assure you that a tip is very well appreciated in this country.

Driving Requirements
Technically speaking, you only need a valid driver's license, passport or a photocopy of one, and registration papers.

194

Heads up!
Flash flash! If a car flashes its lights at you, either your surf boards are about to fall off or there is a cop near by.

Bling Bling! Leaving expensive things like camera equipment and sun glasses in your car rental will get you nowhere but robbed. So, no bling bling!

Corrupt Police In Costa Rica Corrupt road cops are the most common encounter after potholes, but there are no horror stories like in Mexico where they put drugs in your pockets. If you know that you did nothing wrong tell them to piss off or simply let them write you a ticket.

Emergency Bill Keep a ten thousand Colon bill (about $20) no less and NO MORE in case you get in serious trouble for a traffic violation like speeding. Keep Mr. Benjamin out of sight. If you hand one to a cop consider your self stupid.

Carrying Drugs Just don't do it.

Dust in Your Eye Balls (This is my personal request.) When you are driving on dusty roads at high speeds and encounter local pedestrians, please slow down. These people may have already been walking too long under the blistering sun to have an inconsiderate ass shower dust onto them. Please be respectful.

Road Kills Indeed, the roads do kill. Not only are the roads in my country our biggest shame, they are also very dangerous. Always be aware of giant potholes, wild animals, and crazy local drivers.

RADIO STATIONS

9.11   Hip-Hop, rock, house, newer generation style music.
104.3   Similar to 91.1 but less talk in the mornings.
99.5   English classic songs; 80's, 90's etc.
95.5   Jazz, classics, soft, gentle, sleepy music.
90.7   Latin dancing rhythms; Salsa, Merengue, Cumbia etc.
95.5   More Latin music.
93.5   Sports, news, soccer games, soccer games, soccer games, soccer games.
90.3   Classic Boleros; sad, very sad, romantic Spanish rhythms.
97.1   Christian Station.

EMBASSIES

Argentina	(506) 221 3438
Canada	(506) 242 4400
Chile	(506) 224 4243
Denmark	(506) 226 1882
Germany	(506) 232 5533
Israel	(506) 221 6011
Italy	(506) 234 2326
Japan	(506) 232 3787
Mexico	(506) 280 5690
Netherlands	(506) 296 1490
Nicaragua	(506) 222 2373
Panama	(506) 281 2442
Switzerland	(506) 221 4829
U.K.	(506) 258 2025
U.S.A	(506) 220 0053

CONSULATES

Cuba	(506) 291 1614
El Salvador	(506) 257 7855
Finland	(506) 222 6555
Nicaragua	(506) 233 8747
Panama	(506) 281 2104
Sweden	(506) 232 8549
U.S.A.	(506) 220 3050

USEFUL NUMBERS

Emergencies	911
Information	113
Collect Calls	110
Time	112

Jonathan Yonkers and
Ernesto Zúñiga (Jonathan's
younger brother), in front of Hotel
Tamarindo Diria, Tamarindo.
Photos by Thornton Cohen

How to Climb a Coconut Tree

YOU NEED
- A long-sleeve rash guard.
- A spotter.
- A coconut tree.
- Ice bucket and rum (optional).

INSTRUCTIONS
- Tie a knot on the shirt to make a small loop.
- Twist the loop to create a figure 8 and hook each one of your feet into each loop.

- Approach a small coconut tree, placing your strong hand on the back of the tree at shoulder height as if it were a claw, and the other hand in front of you at waist height, as a support.
- Inhale, Exhale, ommmmmm- mmm…
- Jump your feet as high as you can, forcing the bottom part of your feet firmly against the tree (at this point your neck depends on it!). Bring your hands higher; first "The Claw" and then the supporting hand.
- Repeat this motion until you reach the top. Once there, grab a coconut and twist it right off. (The claw stays on the tree while the other hand reaches.)
- Throw the coconuts to your spotter (without hitting him/her on the head!) and go down by way of reversing the steps. First the feet, then the support and at last... the Claw.
- Carefully slice a hole into the coconut (machetes are best for this) and enjoy.
- You can also put the milk in the freezer for 15 minutes and serve ice cold with rum, but DO NOT climb another tree after that!

TIPS

• Make sure you start on a small tree.
• Climbing is easier if the tree is bent.
• Only climb trees that are dry.
• Being in good physical shape decreases your chances of dying in the act.

Warning: Climbing coconut trees is extremely easy, if you are a monkey. Wiping out on a big coconut tree can cause severe injury or death to the climber and to third parties below. Enthusiastic surfers (including surfers trying to impress a female) are advised to try the instructions above only as a way of survival in case of hunger or starvation. Supervision of an experienced Nut is recommended.

Sponsors

Welcome to the world of...

Costa Rica Surf Adventure

ALL INCLUSIVE SURF PACKAGES FOR BEGINNER & ADVANCED SURFEI

WWW·CRSURFADVENTURES·COM

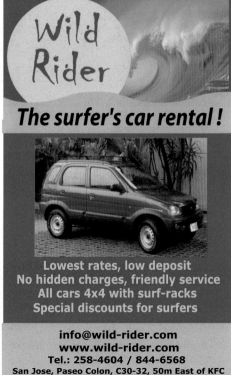

Acknowledgements

Gracias a Dios por permitir que el universo haya conspirado para que este libro se publique, I would also like to thank every person whose name is written in this book, especially all of the photographers and sponsors for their kind contributions. To you for buying this book, I feel very honored and thankful, I hope you like it.

To my professional work team Alex Gesheva and Janet Raftis (copy editors), Monica Schultz (graphic designer), Hector Gamboa (map designer), Alex Núñez (Illustrations). Un millón de gracias.

A mi familia en casa, gracias por siempre apoyarme en mis loqueras.

To Patricia Tomlinson, Miguel and Angela Cleveland, thanks for the financial support; I hope you don't have to break my legs to get your money back!

Rafael Sequeira (alias Eminem) mae, gracias por arreglarme la moto cada vez que se me cacharpea, Tony Chinchilla, gracias por ayudarme a usar la compu y por instalarle programas, buena nota mae! Jimmy Rodríguez por dejarme usar su oficina, Roberto Sibaja, por ideas de ilustraciones, many good! Rafa de Secret Spot, por las ideas buenísimas.

A Eva Rivera, gracias por existir, Tom Clinton in The U.K. (you rock brother!), Steave Cleveland in the U.S., Paco Salmeron y Juan Carlos Lorite en Heredia, gracias muchachos!

First Edition, February 2007
Printed in Costa Rica

*" When you want something, the
whole universe conspires to help
you realize your desire."*

Paulo Coelho

*Positive vibes and enthusiasm
are contagious. Be part of the conspiracy*

www.h2osurftravel.com

Kurt Van Dyke, Kiave, y Odet en Puerto Viejo. Walter "Teka" Fallas en Limon. A Gilbert Brown y todos los Caribbean boays!

Richard Collier, you are perfect example of how the universe conspires! Thank you.

Waylynn Lucas, Alexandra Gruninger, Cristian Jiménez, Guido Saenz en Santa Teresa. Chuck Herwig in Jaco. Andrea Diaz y Juan Vega in Playa Hermosa, Henry Aguilera, Daniel "Tico—Americano", Alvaro Cedeño (guarda vidas en Dominical), ojala nos sigamos pegando buenos tubos en el futuro. Doogie & Rex (Avellanas-Cunucks). Familia Mendoza en Pavones.

To Garret McNamara in Hawaii, Marty Leacy in Australia, Kusru Kama in India, Dennis

Mayo in Atlanta Georgia, Linda, Pete, and Brett Verhoeven in Canada, Kristen Stickels in the U.S., all for causing great positive impact in my life.

Of course my infinite thanks to Christopher and Mary Hatton who were so kind to pick up a stranger who was hitch hiking at night (hungry and cold) out of Matapalo in the Osa Peninsula. God bless you guys.

Gracias a todas las personas que me encontré de camino y que me ayudaron, que Dios los bendiga y les reponga abundante salud y prosperidad.